3—

For Steve Hart —

whose important work
on democratic discourses
I much appreciate,

Robert Fishman

Barcelona — June 3, 2004

Democracy's Voices

Democracy's Voices

Social Ties and the Quality
of Public Life in Spain

Robert M. Fishman

CORNELL UNIVERSITY PRESS
Ithaca and London

First published 2004 by Cornell University Press

Printed in the United States of America

Library of Congress Cataloging-in-Publication Data

Fishman, Robert M., 1955–
  Democracy's voices : social ties and the quality of public life in Spain / Robert M. Fishman.—1st ed.
      p. cm.
Includes bibliographical references and index.
      ISBN 0-8014-4226-5 (cloth : alk. paper)
    1. Political participation—Spain.   2. Democracy—
    Spain.   3. Intellectuals—Spain.   4. Labor leaders—Spain.
    5. Social networks—Spain.   I. Title.
JN8341.F58   2004
306.2′0946—dc22

                                                    2003023061

Cornell University Press strives to use environmentally responsible suppliers and materials to the fullest extent possible in the publishing of its books. Such materials include vegetable-based, low-VOC inks and acid-free papers that are recycled, totally chlorine-free, or partly composed of non-wood fibers. For further information, visit our website at www.cornellpress.cornell.edu.

Cloth printing   10 9 8 7 6 5 4 3 2 1

TO JULIA

AND TO ALL THOSE WHO TAUGHT ME THE VALUE
OF DEMOCRACY'S VOICES, MANY YEARS AGO
IN MORGANTOWN, WEST VIRGINIA

Contents

Acknowledgments

The project that culminated in this book began to take shape in conversations with colleagues and friends at Harvard's Center for European Studies during the late 1980s. George Ross and I developed a working group on consequences of the decline in ties between intellectuals and workers that had taken place in many European societies. In that context I began to sketch out plans for the investigation I began in 1990. Were it not for the fruitful discussions of that group and the encouragement of George, I would never have undertaken the long and methodologically eclectic research path that this book required.

As these pages reflect, I am enormously indebted to the hundreds of local leaders who participated in lengthy interviews during the survey portion of this work. Many of them also took time to discuss the substance of local political and social life during follow-up qualitative fieldwork I undertook in many localities. In a similar vein, numerous Spanish scholars took time to discuss at length the substance of worker–intellectual interactions. Considerations of space, and in some cases of confidentiality, make it impossible for me to list all the individuals whose contributions I deeply appreciate.

By far my greatest institutional debt is to the Center for Advanced Study in the Social Sciences of the Juan March Institute, Madrid. The generous invitation of the Center's founding director, Víctor Pérez Díaz, to spend a year in residence allowed me to design and initiate the survey component of the research in 1990. In addition to offering a stimulating intellectual environment, the Juan March Institute funded my time in Madrid and offered additional support, making the survey possible. A second invitation, to spend the spring semester of 1994 at the Juan March, allowed me to commence the qualitative interviewing and fieldwork. The current director of the Center, José María Maravall, and other scholars there offered valuable insights and support. Maravall, Modesto Escobar, and José Ramón Montero, along with Pérez Díaz, provided extensive comments on an early draft of the survey questionnaire and aided in securing access to leaders to be interviewed. Steven Rosenstone, Alfred Stepan, and Ellen Immergut, fellow visiting scholars at the Center, offered input and encouragement. The administrative director of the Institute, José Luís Yuste, as well as Leopoldo Calvo Sotelo and others in the Juan March's administration, offered consistent and essential support. Crucially, several students and recent graduates of the Center's graduate program assisted in the interviewing.

Despite all this generosity, the task of carrying out a survey in forty-nine municipalities, and following up with extensive qualitative fieldwork, was both daunting and highly time-consuming. To conserve resources and permit the national scope I was determined to achieve, I stitched together and coordinated a network of interviewers, predominantly graduate students in political science and sociology. Antonio Izquierdo, Josep Rodriguez, and Juan Montabes offered contacts among their graduate students, allowing me to build a national network. The group of interviewers I recruited and trained proved to be exceptional in their commitment and skill. Many have subsequently gone on to become scholars in their own right. Considerations of space sadly make it impossible to acknowledge them all, but I do wish to note the extraordinary commitment and contribution to the project of Clemente Penalba Verdú, Fernando Fernández Llébrez, Beatriz Prieto, and Pablo Vázquez de Castro.

The Department of Sociology and the Kellogg Institute of the University of Notre Dame have served as my scholarly home during the work on this project, complemented by the Department of Political and Social Sciences of the Universitat Pompeu Fabra (Barcelona), where I have been a periodic visitor. These settings in which the book took shape have offered an intellectually congenial environment for the analysis of research findings and writing. A fellowship from the German Marshall Fund of the United States and a faculty residential fellowship from the Kellogg Institute supported my writing. Funding from the Kellogg Institute also supported the necessary data entry.

In analyzing data, interpreting qualitative material, and writing, I have been fortunate to draw on extremely helpful commentary from colleagues and friends. For carefully reading and offering extensive comments on an earlier draft of the manuscript I am grateful to Peter Bearman, Suzanne Coshow, David Hachen, Juan Linz, Dan Myers,

Ben Radcliff, and Lyn Spillman. Numerous others offered commentary on specific chapters or chapter segments. In this project, as in my earlier work, I have benefited from the intellectual influence and countless suggestions of Juan Linz and Samuel Valenzuela. Numerous others in South Bend, Barcelona, and the many research settings to which this project took me, generously offered insights and encouragement. In Asturias, Rubén Vega García provided a valuable sense of orientation and numerous introductions. In Barcelona, Francisco Fernandez Buey offered helpful suggestions and encouragement. At Cornell University Press, the rigor and enthusiasm of Roger Haydon have been invaluable. I am also indebted to Louise E. Robbins at the Press and to Kathryn Gohl for their expert editorial suggestions. Nairn Chadwick skillfully prepared the index. Several research assistants have contributed in one way or another to this book; among them I am especially indebted to Suzanne Coshow for technical expertise, scholarly insights, and dedication to the project well beyond what I had any right to expect.

One day while I was on one of many fieldwork visits to the Asturian coalfields of northern Spain, I realized what should, perhaps, have been apparent to me much earlier: The concerns and sensibilities that motivated me to undertake this extensive plan of research were strongly shaped by my experiences growing up in Morgantown, West Virginia—a town that shared some features of many municipalities encompassed by my Spanish research. While I was growing up, my hometown had roughly twenty-five thousand residents, including university faculty and students, industrial workers, and miners working in the surrounding coalfields of northern West Virginia. Conversations between intellectuals and workers, although less common than what I would later find in Spain, were not thoroughly foreign to that environment. In fond memory, I include in this book's dedication my deep appreciation of what I learned in that small Appalachian town.

My greatest debt is to my wife, Julia López, whose love and support helped make my work possible and, even more, deeply enjoyable. Her generous willingness to take time away from her own scholarship to share fully in this project in all ways has been essential. To her, and to those from whom I learned the meaning of political conversations many years ago in Morgantown, West Virginia, I dedicate this book.

ROBERT M. FISHMAN

South Bend, Indiana

1 The Quality of Democracy
Searching for Social Foundations

It doesn't matter if you make a mistake
Or if you're not right,
the only thing that matters
is that you express your opinion.
Speak, express . . .
Write, narrate . . .

Poem from a public school newspaper in the Nalón valley of the Asturian coalfields of northern Spain, as reported by journalist Francisco Palacios in La Nueva España, *May 2, 1994*

In mid-June 1994, at the end of a long and hard-fought election campaign, a political cartoon appeared in a major Barcelona newspaper. The drawing featured a man removing two small objects from his ears, and beside it the caption read: "End of the campaign; out with the earplugs!"[1] The sense of boredom—or even distaste—conveyed by that Barcelona cartoon is not limited to contemporary Spain but can be found, at the turn of the twenty-first century, in numerous countries throughout the world where the tone and substance of politics fail to engage much of the public. Politics, for many citizens, seems more like noise to be blocked out than a debate to be followed with interest. Political discourse strikes many contemporary citizens at the dawn of a new century as empty or narrow rhetoric that is best avoided, thereby undercutting the aspirations of the student poet quoted in this chapter's epigraph, along with those of countless other citizens (and theorists), for whom the expression and interchange of opinions constitute a central objective of democratic life. The hopes of enthusiasts of democracy-as-polis that public life would offer citizens intellectual fulfillment and meaningful engagement seem like visionary musings far removed from the currently dominant mood. By the 1990s, widely voiced complaints about the quality of democratic life had become perhaps the greatest challenge for the future of democratic politics—at least in the perspective of many observers and citizens who as recently as the 1980s were preoccupied with the effort to establish and consolidate new democracies.[2] As Alex Hadenius put the matter in 1997, "the exercise of democracy in the old-established democracies can hardly be judged as inspiring." The compelling need to safeguard existing democracies from the danger of collapse cannot eclipse the enormous contemporary importance of exploring democracy's quality.[3]

In this book I take up the issue of the quality of democratic life. I try to uncover explanations for its deterioration, or at a minimum its shortfall, in places where few observers would think to look. Whereas many analysts would focus on one or another conventional explanation for political outcomes—such as the makeup of official institutions, the behavior (and misbehavior) of politicians themselves, or the changing constraints imposed by the increasingly globalized economy—I instead explore how social ties based in local communities may powerfully shape the nature of democracy's public life.

The concern of many contemporary observers for "the quality of democracy" encompasses various aspects of political life.[4] For Robert Putnam, in *Making Democracy Work*, the fundamental question is how effectively public institutions function, an issue of concern for all political systems.[5] For others, the great determinant of the quality of democracy is best captured by the now classic question, Who gets what from whom? On this understanding, the central issue in the evaluation of democracies is how they deal with distributional questions; judgments about social justice represent the yardstick for measuring the quality of democracy. Without denying the considerable importance of these, and other, basic questions, this book instead places itself in an old but vital tradition that takes political discourse—or if one prefers, political *talk* and deliberation—very seriously, a (quite heterogeneous) tradition that focuses on debate and discussion in the public arena.[6] For numerous theorists—such as Alexis de Tocqueville, John Stuart Mill, and more recently, Hannah Arendt, Jürgen Habermas, and Christoper Lasch as well as many others in the "republican" tradition of democratic theory—a central challenge of formally free societies is the creation of conditions favoring a genuine and lively interchange of perspectives and ideas in the public sphere.[7] The question is not whether a society has encountered a specific solution to challenges of public policy and social justice but whether it affords citizens an engaging public arena within which they may contemplate, discuss if they wish, and ultimately choose among competing views, alternatives, and proposals. For these theorists as well as, in a somewhat different vein, for the Italian Marxist theoretician Antonio Gramsci, the mere existence of an elected government does not guarantee the public advocacy of alternatives, and thus lively and engaging debate. For a substantial number of influential thinkers, the quality of democracy rests not only on the effectiveness of institutions, the nature of distributional outcomes, and the level of conventional political participation but also on the tenor and range of public discourse. I take as a given that free and competitive democratic elections, and the accompanying legal guarantees of freedom, are *necessary* for political actors to construct a lively public sphere, but the basic institutional framework of contemporary democracy is no *guarantee* that a society will attain that goal. This book addresses a fundamental problem: the ability of society to offer citizens an engaging choice among meaningful alternatives—and thus a debate that can be followed with interest— instead of mere noise in the public arena.

The greatest orators and motivators of collective political energies often take the tack of Abraham Lincoln in his extraordinary Gettysburg Address, in which he saluted the contribution of deeds, in the decisive battle fought on that spot, and minimized the importance of words, especially his own: "The world will little note, nor long remember what we say here, but it can never forget what they did here." But as Garry Wills argues in his analysis of that enduring speech, "The power of words has rarely been given a more compelling demonstration." "The Civil War *is*, to most Americans, what Lincoln wanted it to *mean*. Words had to complete the work of guns."[8] As Wills contends, words can prove as memorable as deeds and speeches as significant as armed conflict in the shaping of political life. The great antislavery cause of the nineteenth century generated enduring words as well as historic battles; both debate and armed confrontation mark the central episode of the American nineteenth century.

The opposition of words to deeds may prove on occasion rhetorically convenient, suggesting that the relevance of one diminishes or even fully eclipses the significance of the other. Yet that opposition is a false one; in reality both words and deeds are essential in the

conduct of public life, not only in moments of great historical confrontation but also in times of relative normalcy. Thus I make no
assumption here that words take precedence over deeds; my simple
premise is that words and debate, as well as policies and deeds, help
afford politics with the meaning and the interest many citizens hope
to find in public life. Just as the nature of policies differs from one
political unit to another, so too does the shape or quality of public
rhetorics. The reader will not find among the declarations of the
many local leaders examined here assertions or arguments as memorable as those of historical giants such as Abraham Lincoln, but the
political and rhetorical energies of local leaders are decisively important in the ability of Spain—or any country—to meet the challenge
of offering citizens a debate among alternatives rather than mere
noise in the public arena. Wars that expand human freedom and
speeches as deeply compelling as the address at Gettysburg are
extraordinary historical exceptions, but even in ordinary times the
rhetoric of lesser-known leaders affords to simple local struggles
widely diverging understandings, and thus a wide variety of connections between those local efforts and broader objectives or processes.
The rhetorics expressed in the course of local struggles provide citizens—both within their locality and far beyond its borders—with a
way of making sense out of such political action, a way of determining whether the endeavor is threatening, liberating, or perhaps
simply lacking in interest. Thus I am concerned here not with the
simple existence of locally generated conflicts but with the interest
and meaning they may acquire for the broad public through the discourse of local leaders.

That the bonds, or ties, among people make a difference in social
and political life is a core idea of sociology.[9] Alexis de Tocqueville,
in his classic works on the United States and on France, observed
that the prevalence of connections among citizens varied enormously
from one society to another with highly significant consequences:
where social bonds were prevalent, as in the United States, collective
endeavors among like-minded persons were common and debate
among alternatives characterized public life; where social bonds
were weak (or, more precisely, infrequent), as in France, collective
endeavors were rare in normal times and opinions were often left
unexpressed.[10] A paucity of social ties generated an impoverished
public life, a democracy lacking genuinely free expression and debate.
For Tocqueville and many political analysts who have followed him,

the most fundamentally important social bonds are those established by formal associations of various sorts.[11] Bowling leagues, business associations, feminist organizations, local improvement clubs, and political parties are only a few of the many types of associations emphasized by neo-Tocquevillean analysts.

A somewhat different tradition in sociology provides equal or greater emphasis to the frequently informal ties among individuals and the social networks generated by such ties. What really matters in this line of analysis is the presence of bonds among people, whether they are expressed in friendship, mere acquaintanceship, family ties, *or* joint participation in an organization. Social ties, as emphasized in this more recent line of scholarship, may be found *outside* as well as *within* the formal organizations emphasized by the Tocquevilleans.[12] Moreover, for analysts of social networks, indirect ties carry a powerful significance in social life; one treats the friends of one's friends in a different manner from the enemies of one's friends. The relevance of this far more elaborate understanding of social connections for historically crucial political episodes has been developed in pioneering works by Peter Bearman and Roger Gould.[13] The sociological understanding of how politics may be reshaped by the changing face of social connections has also inspired more synthetic overviews of American politics such as the stimulating work of Lasch.

This book draws on both the Tocquevillean and the more conventionally sociological traditions, searching for insights and, even more importantly, research questions suggested by these two perspectives. I examine ties found within organizations as well as the bonds among friends. On the basis of my research findings, I explore briefly a key Tocquevillean theme: direct effects of local associational life on the quality of democracy. But the major question I pose concerns the impact of certain social ties—between intellectuals and local working-class leaders—without restricting the analysis on the basis of the ties' social context, be it institutional or informal. Both linkages within formal organizations and bonds located outside such settings ought to be, at least in principle, of potential interest. The data and local experiences presented in this book suggest that those who focus almost exclusively on formal organizations such as parties, unions, or local cultural associations err in doing so. I identify, with the firm grounding of empirical research findings, substantial consequences of this broader understanding of social ties for democracy's public rhetorics. However, I make no effort here to rigorously explore the overall structure and significance of extensive networks built on indirect as well as direct ties. In short, I attempt to determine whether the quality of public life bears the mark of the ordinary decisions we all make about the persons and groups with whom we speak, interact, and form friendships. Thus I pose a simple but fundamental question about contemporary democracy, one that stands outside the terrain typically explored by political analysts: To what extent does the deterioration or reinvigoration of public life—its tendency to disengage or engage citizens—rest on forms of social life to which we often attach little or no *political* significance?

I focus here on bonds between two specific social groups—intellectuals and workers, or working-class leaders—whose interrelations, in the arguments of a long and distinguished theoretical tradition, have been fundamental to the shape of politics in many national settings.[14] Although the data we shall examine focus heavily on those specific ties, the argument I advance is broader in its scope. I conceive of ties such as those here examined as but one example of a broad array of social relations among citizens that carry important political consequences, and thus the argument developed in the following chapters generalizes beyond the data directly analyzed. Nonetheless, the empirical core of the book rests squarely on intellectual–worker ties.

It may seem odd to many readers, and particularly to those in the English-speaking world, to expect to find significant linkages between intellectuals and workers, but in Spain, and indeed throughout the Latin European world, such ties enjoy a long and vital tradition.[15] Many proponents and critics alike of the ideological style of politics characteristic of Latin Europe during most of the twentieth century attribute considerable importance to the relations between intellectuals and workers when discussing overall explanations for the form taken by national political life. My focus on the impact of bonds between these two groups follows not only from that theoretical tradition but even more importantly from impressions, intuitions, and above all, unanswered questions formed during my earlier fieldwork in Spain.[16] What has ended up as the central argument of this book began as a set of questions with no specific preconceived answers, although my general expectation that the answers would prove interesting has not been disappointed. Building on those earlier fieldwork experiences, the anthropological sensibility that led me to ask questions I felt crucial has been a constant source of intellectual energy, and curiosity, in the research underpinning this book. Nonetheless, I constantly strive in these pages to build interpretations and arguments solidly grounded in rigorous, and often quantitative, empirical analysis.

Theoretical Underpinnings

Two theorists, Alexis de Tocqueville and Antonio Gramsci, with partially overlapping concerns but widely divergent lines of argument, have proved enormously suggestive in the conception of this book. For Tocqueville, the Frenchman of aristocratic origins whose ideas have fascinated Americans on both the right and the left of the political center, a fundamental problem in the modern world is that, paradoxically, social equality and formally democratic institutions offer no guarantee for the existence of genuine political liberty. Both the public expression of varied opinions and joint action by those sharing common objectives or grievances may be undermined, argues Tocqueville, by the overpowering influence of majority sentiment and the institutional weight of a strong central state. Modern democracy, in the absence of certain crucial attributes capable of sustaining public life, may suffer from a weak citizenry composed of isolated and quiescent individuals. These weak citizens live in a political world lacking meaningful public debate and significant collective endeavors. Grievances may remain unexpressed—at least in public.[17] The remedy for this syndrome, Tocqueville asserts, rests on foundations present in the United States: strong civic or political associations and administratively powerful local governments, along with a host of other specific features of America, enable citizens to act and to speak publicly on the basis of their own sentiments, even if this places them at odds with majority opinion or the central state.

For Tocqueville, the local community is the arena crucial to the vitality of democratic life. Public debate and political freedom for the nation as a whole are sustained by the autonomous voices and efforts of citizens in their municipalities. A vibrant public life, with a multiplicity of views, rests on the ability of people to speak and act locally. The initiative and autonomy required if local communities are to animate public life rest, in turn, on social and political arrangements at the municipal level. Tocqueville's fundamental question about the sustainability of genuine liberty in modern democracy emphasizes heavily the importance of locally based arrangements: Do people form common bonds and act collectively through associations and local government, or do they remain quiescent and isolated from one another, allowing the central government and nationally predominant ideas to shape all meaningful political outcomes?

Antonio Gramsci, the early-twentieth-century Italian Communist whose theoretical writings have proved highly suggestive to numerous non-Marxists as well as Marxists, like Tocqueville searched out a basis in society for voices and perspectives that contest dominant, or "hegemonic," ideas.[18] Gramsci focused on the ability of ideas, when defended in a widespread fashion by persons located in strategic positions within society and culture, to prove as significant as raw "power" in determining the course of politics and history. He called this social power based on the dissemination and broad acceptance of ideas "hegemony": the hegemony enjoyed by those whose ideas are widely accepted was for Gramsci an objective as important as the conquest of state power had been for Lenin. The crucial social relationship, in the Gramscian scheme, is the linkage between intellectuals and other social actors, whether they are workers, peasants, business leaders, or whomever. The presence throughout society—in schools, neighborhoods, workplaces, and so on—of "organic" intellectuals tied to a specific social group would provide that group with hegemony, or at least with a reasonable share of hegemony.

Thus in the Gramscian vision, intellectuals assume vital significance in the emergence and diffusion of alternatives to dominant ideas and interests. But it is precisely through their social linkages, commitments, and placement in the fabric of collective life that intellectuals are able to afford the polity with alternative visions. It is the social relations of intellectuals rather than the intrinsic power of their ideas that allow them to meaningfully challenge dominant ideas and interests.

Tocqueville, as well, viewed intellectuals as potentially powerful players in setting a society's political and discursive landscape, yet he viewed with concern their engagement in politics. Tocqueville celebrated, above all, pragmatic locally oriented politics; the grand concerns and abstract visions of intellectuals, he argued, represented a dangerous alternative to the virtues of a practically minded local politics. At best they might distort the vibrant pragmatism of local life and at worst they could generate radicalized and destabilizing confrontation. Intellectuals occupied a key place in what he portrayed as the highly unsatisfactory arrangement of social and political life in France.[19] Their relative absence from public life in the United States represented, by way of contrast in his comparative formulation, one element of America's more felicitous arrangement of social and political interaction.

The implicit debate between Tocqueville and Gramsci offers us a stimulating starting point for exploring the impact of social ties (such as those linking intellectuals to workers) on the quality of democratic life. Both theorists are concerned with the conditions that encourage the emergence and public communication of one or more alternatives to dominant ideas. Granted, for Tocqueville the danger is what he terms the "tyranny of the majority," whereas for Gramsci the issue is hegemony in class relations. But despite these terminological differences, and more significant underlying theoretical (and political) disparities, both writers' fundamental search focuses on conditions that generate—or undercut—a public challenge to dominant opinions and ideas. That search leads both theorists to explore social arrangements in local or, in any event, fairly microlevel settings. Here, however, the similarities end. For Tocqueville, civil and political associations, as well as administratively powerful municipal governments, offer the best guarantees of public contestation. Gramsci, concerned specifically with the ability of subordinate social groups to challenge dominant ideas and interests, placed his trust instead in the existence of a network of politically oriented intellectuals linked to other actors in a wide array of social settings, such as neighborhoods, schools, and workplaces. Tocqueville, fearful of an ideologically oriented politics, viewed with trepidation the involvement of intellectuals in politics. Thus, although the two theorists celebrated fundamentally different social arrangements, the problems on which they reflected and the places to which they looked for answers overlapped sufficiently to pose interesting questions for our exploration. Social reality may well be quite different from what both theorists envisioned, but their ideas jointly pose major questions and help suggest avenues of exploration.

Many other social analysts have theorized broadly about the place of intellectuals in politics, and in some instances specifically about ties between intellectuals and labor.[20] A common view of both enthusiasts and critics of radicalized working-class action is that left-wing intellectuals have been partially responsible for the ideological opposition of labor to capitalism in some national or historical settings. In this line of reasoning, intellectuals lead workers to embrace a radical rejection of existing social relations; where intellectuals are absent from the ranks of labor, working-class moderation is seen as the likely outcome. In a sense, this line of reasoning loosely echoes themes in both Tocqueville and Gramsci. Otherwise dissimilar social thinkers have shared the assumption that where intellectuals are tightly bound up in a political movement, they will provide that movement with an abstract or generalizing vision that frames its central objectives. Yet despite the theoretical appeal of this argument, the empirical case for it has not been adequately made. My research makes it possible to assess this claim, although my primary focus remains centered on public discourse and the quality of democratic life.

At some point in the late twentieth century, probably during the 1980s, previously close or frequent contacts between labor and politically sympathetic intellectuals began to wane in several countries in Latin Europe and elsewhere. In the U.S. case, which is far removed from the Spanish context analyzed here, analysts have written of "a wall of mutual suspicion and recrimination [that] has virtually terminated any communication between these two worlds."[21] This decline in the historically and (in many national cases) politically important bonds between workers and intellectuals, to some degree the result of the disenchantment of many intellectuals with classic ideologies of the Left, encouraged many observers to perceive a growing "divorce" between these two social actors.[22] My effort in this book to ascertain the impact on democracy's public arena of ties between workers and intellectuals was partly motivated by that perception. My research also makes it possible to delineate in rough form the prevalence of those ties and their tendency to decline, or gain, in strength for specific segments of labor.

Settings, Actors, Definitions

The Spanish Case: Contextualizing Democracy's Quality

In this volume I explore social underpinnings of the quality of democratic life through extensive empirical material, both survey-based and qualitative in nature, collected at the local level in Spain. I endeavor to address issues of broad theoretical and practical significance from the vantage point provided by this empirical material, but I also take seriously the Spanish case and, where appropriate, its distinctive features or challenges. I take up, in chapter 6, the issue of how well, and how far, this book's findings travel beyond the Spanish case. As I attempt to show there, the causal dynamics here outlined are likely to be found in many contexts outside the Spanish case, but not in all contexts. Context matters. This book offers a generalizing argument that fully heeds that fact.

For several reasons Spain offers us an especially fruitful setting to take up the question of democratic quality. The Spanish case has assumed enormous importance in the scholarly writing on democracy and its alternatives. And in a more directly practical sense, at various points in the twentieth century, the country's collective experiences have attracted broad international attention among the politically active, especially during the Civil War (1936–39) and the post-Franco transition to democracy beginning in 1975.[23] In the academic literatures on the breakdown of democracies, the conceptualization of nondemocratic regimes, and transitions to democracy, the Spanish case has assumed paradigmatic importance. The seminal contributions of Spanish political sociologist Juan Linz, whose work is typically global in scope but with Spain constantly present as a salient point of reference, may help explain this scholarly prominence, but only in part.[24] Many other social scientists and political actors have also taken Spain as a case of special significance, helping to elucidate patterns of broadly comparative import. Thus, for example, for political scientist Richard Gunther, Spain's approach to democratic transition offers "the very model of the modern elite settlement," a pattern later identified by Gunther and other analysts in many national cases of democratic transition. Writing from a substantially different perspective in their recent wide-ranging study of "contentious politics," Doug McAdam, Sidney Tarrow, and Charles Tilly focused on the Spanish case as one of only a handful of national experiences examined in their discussion of modern democratization.[25] Many comparative and theoretical arguments in the scholarly analysis of politics have emerged from discussions initially focused on Spain.

Yet despite the considerable hopes historically placed on Spanish democracy, and the enthusiasm of many scholars and political actors for the largely consensus- and reform-oriented Spanish model of regime transition, the post-Franco system has not been without its substantial disappointments, some of them emblematic of deficits in democratic quality perceived to exist in numerous other contemporary cases.[26] Support for democracy as a system has been consistently very high throughout the post-Franco period, but that has not precluded the widespread expression of disenchantment with various aspects of democratic political life.[27] The Barcelona cartoon mentioned in this chapter's opening lines, bemoaning the boredom generated by a recent electoral campaign, is but one small manifestation of such sentiments. Most Spaniards support democracy, but many among them feel more or less disillusioned with the public life they experience. In discussing such "disenchantment," scholars have chosen to emphasize rather different features of the political system. In his highly suggestive and wide-ranging analysis *The Return of Civil Society*, sociologist Víctor Pérez Díaz notes with concern "the emergence of traditions in the sphere of public debate which are quite worrisome," leading him to decry "a systematic distortion of the public sphere."[28] His concerns include the disjunction between much political rhetoric and actual programmatic alternatives. Taking a rather different approach, political scientists Peter McDonough, Samuel Barnes, and Antonio López Pina emphasize, in their data-rich discussion, that "two types of civic engagement and political interaction—membership in voluntary associations and conventional political participation—are exceptionally low in Spain."[29] More recent analysts of Spanish politics, often with a firm foundation in survey data, continue to focus on the phenomenon of "disaffection."[30] In his important comparative analysis of political disaffection, Mariano Torcal found, on the basis of 1999 data for nine countries, that Spanish citizens were those least likely to claim "a pretty good understanding of the important political issues."[31] Thus there is ample reason to examine empirical evidence on the social determinants of public discourse in a democracy that has proved disappointing to many, despite the hopes initially placed in it.

Our search for underpinnings of democratic quality, or its absence, in working-class communities and contexts rests, in part, on an extraordinary paradox of the Spanish case: although the transition to democracy involved widespread moderation and restraint, incorporating labor as well as other collective actors, and in spite of the extraordinarily low formal membership currently enjoyed by unions, democratic Spain consistently stands out as an international leader in labor conflict as well as the leader in European statistics on strikes.

TABLE 1.1
Labor conflict in the European Union, 1990–95

Rank	Country	Average No. Days Not Worked
1	Spain	319.43
2	Finland	210.80
3	Italy	146.95
4	Ireland	100.71
5	Sweden	67.0
6	Denmark	39.29
7	The Netherlands	29.24
8	United Kingdom	28.69
9	Belgium	26.47
10	Portugal	25.25
11	France	20.70

Source: International Labor Organization, LABORSTA Database, tables 2A and 9C. Measure is based on dividing the total number of days not worked by the total labor force and averaging for the period 1990–95.
Note: Greece is not included because of missing values.

During the years 1990–95, Spain stood as the European Union member state with the highest level of labor conflict, as reported in table 1.1.[32] The Spanish tendency toward exceptionally high labor conflict has been a consistent feature of the country's post-Franco democracy.

This pattern suggests an interesting puzzle in the Spanish case: How is it that democracy's public sphere often elicits disappointment, and disengagement, despite the high level of popular energy directed toward the collective expression of grievances? This query raises, in turn, a second and unavoidable question: Is it possible that much of Spain's collective protest ends up *disengaging*, rather than *engaging*, large segments of the public? The answer may be found, in large measure, in the initiatives and discourse of labor. I shall identify and attempt to account for sharply differing claims on the public's attention emanating from working-class communities and actors. The differences on which I focus, and that carry major lessons extending well beyond the industrial contexts studied, are unrelated to the conventional distinction between radicalism and moderation.

The nature of public debate assumed special importance in the Spanish case both before and during the time in which the research discussed here was conducted for one additional reason: the Partido Socialista Obrero Español (PSOE), the Spanish Socialist Party, held governmental power in Madrid from late 1982 through early 1996, and for much of that time its political dominance seemed so great that some political observers openly fretted over the danger of "PRI-ification" of the party, a reference to the suffocating electoral and governmental hegemony held for decades by Mexico's Partido Rev-olucionario Institucional. This fear, in its full-blown version, vastly overstated the PSOE's dominance and undervalued the democratic resilience of Spanish society, but nonetheless it focused attention on the sources of public contestation challenging the Socialist Party's predominance.

Perhaps surprisingly, for readers unfamiliar with this period of Spanish political history, working-class communities and organiza-tions constituted a major source of contestation to the Socialist government in Madrid. Although distinguished scholars have emphasized the social democratic, and thus left-oriented, compo-nents of PSOE policies, other analysts and observers have instead highlighted disjunctions between the policies of PSOE Prime Minis-ter Felipe González and traditional social democratic or socialist agendas or have actually portrayed the policies of the González era as more favorable toward business and hostile toward labor than those of the previous center-right government of the (now defunct) Unión del Centro Democrático.[33] Spanish citizens, along with schol-arly experts, have disagreed over the record of thirteen and a half years of PSOE rule. For many Spaniards, González was a towering and charismatic figure whose governments achieved many practical successes in addition to their repeated electoral victories. The skills and dedication of the PSOE's most impressive leaders and govern-mental ministers unquestionably fostered that positive reading. However, for many other Spaniards the frequent debate-impeding insistence of González that his government's positions represented "the only possible policy," coupled with increasing instances of corruption, contributed to a perceived deterioration of the public arena.

In this context, the two main union confederations and political forces to the left of González assumed increasing importance in artic-ulating opposition. The large general strike in December 1988, led by the socialist-oriented Unión General de Trabajadores (UGT) and the communist-oriented Comisiones Obreras (CCOO), reinforced the sense that labor constituted a major base of contestation to PSOE policies at a time when no party seemed likely to displace the Socialists from governmental power. It is hardly surprising that one of the union leaders I interviewed in 1994 insisted that "the unionism of CCOO is the opposition."[34] As in any democracy, the electoral performance of parties and politicians ultimately proved decisive in shaping the direction of governmental power, and in March 1996 the PSOE lost its majority as a result of the ascendance of the victorious right-of-center Partido Popular (PP) and the defection of many left-of-center voters to the postcommunist alliance Izquierda Unida (IU). It is noteworthy that the high point of electoral support for Spanish postcommunists (or communists) came in 1996, long after communism had ceased to offer Spanish workers and left-oriented voters a compelling systemic alternative. This electoral result, which helped undermine PSOE dominance, clearly represented a critique of the González government. Thus working-class communities, organizations, and voters played a crucial oppositional role in a time of perceived party hegemony. My research question concerns the voices that emerged from working-class contexts, in this historical setting, and their impact, whether positive or not, on democracy's public arena.

I make no assumption that working-class voices necessarily contributed positively to the public arena in this context. My only assumption, underpinned by both strike and electoral data, is that those voices *mattered* and that their shape or tenor therefore merits careful study.

The Research Strategy

I have focused my research efforts on the local level, carrying out both a survey and qualitative interviewing in numerous industrial working-class communities throughout Spain. The survey interviews were conducted with local working-class leaders in forty-nine industrial municipalities with populations greater than 25,000. After analyzing the survey results, I returned to many of the communities to carry out qualitative interviews; it has proved highly useful to make numerous repeat visits to the localities of greatest interest. The combination of qualitative and survey research findings has made it possible to address the questions that motivated this study in a fashion that neither research technique, standing on its own, would have permitted.

The research focus on leaders and social relations based in local settings follows, in part, the theoretical arguments of Tocqueville and Gramsci; both thinkers stress the importance of localized social relations in generating a contested and thus lively—or, where absent, a moribund—public sphere of discussion. The approach followed here also reflects the understanding of labor organization and the research strategy I developed in the course of my earlier work on unions and democratic transition in Spain: local leaders represent a distinctive layer of sociopolitical organization, and they contribute in frequently underappreciated ways to developments and outcomes that attract broad attention.[35] The actions they initiate, the risks they assume, and frequently the very views they hold differentiate them from both national leaders and the rank and file. In the absence of clear and context-specific evidence, one can never assume that local leaders and the rank and file think—and speak—in precisely the same tones. Those who lead and initiate local actions are by definition local leaders, be they formal, that is to say, official leaders, or informal, that is, extra-official leaders. Moreover, as more than a generation of scholarship has shown, underlying public concerns and interests may be activated and articulated in very different ways, depending on the perspectives and agendas of the organizations and leaders representing those concerns and interests.

The shortage of individuals willing—and able—to serve as leaders at the local level is a fundamentally important constraint for collective action, although it is typically not appreciated as such.[36] Points of view and political alternatives that are widely visible at the national level are completely absent in some local settings, not necessarily because no one present is predisposed to support those points of view but rather because no one is willing to serve as a local leader by raising the flag and presenting the case publicly for that perspective, be it right-wing or left-wing Catholicism, reformist postcommunism, conservative nationalism, Trotskyism, or whatever.

Frequently within specific places of work, and to a somewhat lesser extent within towns, the willingness—or unwillingness—of persons present to serve as local leaders for one or another perspective decisively shapes the local configuration of viewpoints on political and labor issues. If there are no reformist postcommunist leaders available, that perspective will not be offered locally, even if in principle some of those living or working in the local context would be willing to support but not lead that current of opinion. So too with right-wing or left-wing versions of social democracy, and any other perspective for that matter. The shape of local politics is determined in part by the (always limited) pool of persons willing and able to serve as local leaders. Leaders help to generate local patterns of public life precisely because the choices they make, the causes they defend, the political style they adopt—all of these things—afford the political arena with a shape it would not have absent their efforts (or the efforts of other local leaders sharing their perspective). One cannot safely assume that causes, demands, and collective strategies will be publicly defended simply because they represent one possible way of articulating local interests. In any given locality, some of the theoretically possible ways to defend local interests will fail to make their appearance. When it comes to explaining the presence or absence of any one given form of politics or way of defending shared interests, there is a simple rule of thumb: no local leadership, no local appearance. Thus the observable differences among localities in the ways they address political concerns and articulate their interests reflect in part variations in the behavior and the outlook of the leaders to be found in those localities. We shall soon see that seemingly similar towns often defend their interests in very different ways. Local leaders and the social ties that help account for their behavior contribute powerfully to generating those differences.

Another fundamental reason to focus this inquiry on local leaders is that the social ties here explored are especially problematic, that is, particularly subject to variability, at this level. National leaders of labor always have available to them avenues of contact and opportunities for interchange with intellectuals, although the intensity of these relations and the importance placed in them clearly vary a good deal from one individual case to another. Rank-and-file workers, on the other hand, are unlikely to sustain relations with intellectuals, except where authors or scholars who originate in a working-class environment maintain family or friendship ties with workers among whom they grew up. In contrast, among local working-class leaders, be they union or party officials, relations with intellectuals are reasonably frequent but still cannot be taken for granted. Ties at this level are substantially more prevalent than among rank-and-file workers but less so than among national leaders. Thus it is possible systematically to compare local leaders who maintain ties to intellectuals with others who do not. Through this comparison we can assess the causal impact of the ties: Are leaders who participate in interactions with intellectuals different from others who do not, and if so, why? Answering this question and linking the answer to the overall quality of democratic life have not been easy, but the survey interviews with local leaders in industrial communities allow multiple avenues of analysis. The qualitative interviews I have carried out in many of the same localities after examining the survey results have made it possible to connect the predispositions highlighted by the survey to relevant local histories that reflect how politics actually takes place in these settings.

Defining Intellectuals

It would be unwise to theorize about intellectuals, or to explore the impact of their relations with workers, without establishing clearly what is meant by the term. Numerous definitions are possible, and although no single one of them is fully satisfactory, it was necessary to define the term clearly in the questionnaire I developed for the survey; otherwise, respondents would have used many different understandings of *intellectual* in their answers. Given divergent understandings among the respondents, comparisons of the responses would prove misleading: a union leader who thinks of all high school teachers as intellectuals would be likely to report many more contacts than would another who conceives of only internationally famous philosophers as intellectuals, even if the actual experiences of the two were highly similar.

The primary definition of *intellectual* employed here, the one used explicitly in the survey's line of questioning about intellectuals, identifies this group as the set of "authors who write for an educated or general audience—whether in books or magazines; of recognized artists; and of university professors." I focus through this specification on the group of persons occupying socially recognized positions as (secular) interpreters of reality.[37] Of course many of the individuals who occupy such positions are not particularly "intellectual." Many readers of this book surely know of university professors, and authors, who care relatively little about ideas or knowledge. But the social position they occupy, as professors or authors, is one typically assumed to be intellectual in nature.

The Gramscian conception of *intellectual*, also of great relevance in this book, focuses instead on the degree to which people actually interpret and theorize the social world. I address this conception in the survey by asking respondents a series of questions about *theorists*, a term defined in the interviews as "persons who do not limit themselves to commenting and acting on immediate and concrete aspects of political and union life but who look for broader forms of analysis and explanation to understand political, economic and social reality." Clearly, local leaders and activists can qualify as theorists by this definition, even if the position they occupy in the social order is not widely conceived of as an intellectual one. As we shall see, both "intellectuals" and "theorists" play a role in the social realities here analyzed. Many readers would doubtless prefer a slightly different use of these terms. Because my objective in this book is to examine the political consequences of given *social ties*, and not to engage in a (perhaps important) lengthy conceptual debate, I have chosen to resolve the terminological issue quickly before turning to empirical concerns. I trust that the findings made possible by this approach are likely to prove of considerable interest even to most of those readers who would have preferred a somewhat different set of terminological choices.

The Leaders Interviewed

Those interviewed in the industrial communities included both institutional and extra-institutional leaders of workers. The initial design called for four individuals, the secretaries general of the two main worker-oriented parties and the two main unions, to be interviewed. The organizations represented by these respondents, the PSOE, Partido Comunista de España (PCE) or IU (in Catalonia the Partit dels Socialistes de Catalunya [PSC-PSOE], and the Partit Socialista Unificat de Catalunya [PSUC] or IC), CCOO, and UGT all have a major national presence and were, with few exceptions, institutionally relevant at the local level as well. The initial four respondents were then asked to suggest several names of individuals of real importance for the collective life of workers in their locality. These names formed the basis for a "snowball" sample that widened the study to include extra-institutional as well as institutional leaders. Up to four additional people, chosen through the snowball technique, were interviewed within each town.

The case I make in this book is based on a thorough analysis of two very different types of interviews carried out over a period of several years. The analytical basis for the argument advanced here rests largely on a survey of just over three hundred local leaders in the sampled towns. The questionnaire I developed for this purpose was lengthy and composed mainly, but not exclusively, of closed-ended questions. The interviews lasted a minimum of one hour and a quarter and usually a good deal longer. The survey afforded the opportunity for quantitative analysis aimed at uncovering and demonstrating causal linkages among the variables of interest. However, many of the items included in the survey are especially useful for exploring predispositions and broadly held attitudes. It is difficult, on the basis of a survey alone, to establish how those pre-dispositions are translated into the real substance of political life. The survey clearly shows the existence of major differences among the respondents, differences that can be substantially explained by the shape of their social ties, especially with intellectuals. Are these differences real, that is, are they reflected in the way politics actu-ally takes place at the local level, or are they merely an artifact of the survey methodology itself? I was not satisfied that my research was complete until I had gathered the material necessary to adequately answer that question. If the differences are real, then it should be pos-sible to identify them in comparisons among local communities and in the examination of paths they choose to follow in defending their interests. To address this concern I carried out a number of qualita-tive interviews in the communities where the survey was conducted. Where possible, the qualitative interviews compared communities similar to one another in most conventional terms but markedly dif-ferent from one another in the pattern of their linkages to intellec-tuals. The most telling of these comparisons contrasts the two mining valleys of Asturias, the Nalón and the Caudal, showing how dissimilar patterns of ties to intellectuals have helped generate markedly different strategies—and rhetorics—for defending the inter-ests of miners and other residents of the valleys.

Towns and Regions

The towns studied in this book include almost all the communi-ties in Spain with more than 25,000 inhabitants and in which the industrial working class predominates numerically. Several regional restrictions, however, were placed on the sample of municipalities. Localities in the Basque Country and Galicia were excluded from the study because the intertwining of regional-national and class identities in those two contexts would have made it necessary to substantially reformulate both the research design and the set of questions that proved meaningful for the rest of Spain. The greatest industrial region in Spain, Catalonia, has—like the Basque Country and Galicia—a distinctive language and national identity, but in crucial respects Catalonia resembles patterns of political association found throughout Spain; thus Catalonia has been included here.[38] In Catalonia, workers are represented in both the union and party arenas by organizations that form part (with some qualifications) of the nationwide unions and parties that represent workers throughout Spain. Whereas regional-nationalist unions are extremely important in the Basque Country and are relevant—but less so—in Galicia, Catalan nationalist unions are virtually absent from Catalonia. In the study of organized working-class politics, the Basque Country and to a lesser extent Galicia virtually require separate monographic treatment. Catalonia, in contrast, can be easily incorporated into a study of nationwide patterns of political life—albeit with sensitivity to the specificities and the national identity of the Catalans.

The number of industrial communities is so great in Catalonia that in the initial selection of towns to be studied, twenty-six were in Catalonia out of an overall total of fifty-four municipalities. This great presence of Catalan towns in the sample reflected not only the industrial strength of the Catalan context but also the urban structure of the Barcelona metropolitan area. The majority of the residents of Greater Barcelona live in medium-sized and even small-sized cities surrounding the central municipality. In contrast, in Greater Madrid the majority of the population lives within the city limits of Madrid itself. This difference reflects in part the aggressive annexation policy of Madrid, which has incorporated many surrounding towns into the municipal boundaries of the national capital. But regardless of how we choose to explain this difference, the implications for the sample of towns were clear: the urban structure of greater Barcelona threatened to generate an overrepresentation of Catalonia in the sample. As a simple solution to this problem, the five communities immediately contiguous to Barcelona itself were excluded. This still left twenty-one Catalan municipalities in the overall sample of forty-nine towns, with many of them located in the Greater Barcelona metropolitan area but none of them directly adjacent to the area's principal municipality.

The criterion for including the forty-nine towns was a simple one. Municipalities in which industrial workers represented a majority of the labor force in the 1981 census (the most recent census for which data were available at the municipal level at the time when the selection of towns was made) were chosen. All towns whose population was greater than 25,000 and met this criterion were included, with the geographic restrictions mentioned earlier. The objective was simple: to include all the municipalities in which local working-class leaders were likely to be central players in political and associational life.

Why the exclusive emphasis on working-class communities? Workers, their organizations, and their leaders represent only one among the many fundamental sets of actors in political life. All of these actors—from successful (or failed) Internet entrepreneurs to the guardians of traditional values and the advocates of autonomy for marginal subcultures—form part of the great festival of democracy, unless they succumb to apolitical indifference. There is no assumption here that workers and their organizations are more important for democracy's spirit and substance than are such other groups. But I do assume that workers and their organizations remain a fundamentally important part of a system based on political equality freely expressed at the ballot box. If one wishes to understand working-class politics and its ability or inability to contribute to the overall quality of democratic life, then clearly one has to look for working-class politics where one is likely to find it, and that is what I have done. Focusing on working-class environments, I explore the behavior of a collectivity that generates much social protest in Spain but that may or may not contribute to the quality of democratic public life. I assume that social protest by workers or others may broaden and deepen the public arena of debate, or that such protest may contribute, instead, to a collective sense of exhaustion with narrow and disruptive actions that fail to engage the larger public. Both scenarios are at least theoretically possible. Importantly, as well, the *similarities* among many of the towns in the problems they face make it possible to explore systematically explanations for the *differences* that emerge among them. Many of the conclusions drawn from this study are likely applicable to non-working-class environments.

The towns I have studied (identified in fig. 1.1) are in numerous respects quite unlike one another, despite their common placement in the dimension of social structure used to select them. A sensitive observer or thoughtful traveler would likely think it odd to group under one comprehensive conceptual heading—to analyze together as if they represented a meaningful unit—towns so seemingly different as the forty-nine localities on which I focus. From sun-baked Elche, with its extraordinarily dense palm groves (which have exported date palms to the Arab world for replanting) and its largely hidden shoe industry to the classically industrial mining and factory town of Langreo, surrounded by the green hills of the Nalón valley in Asturias, the contrasts are indeed immense. Some of the towns, such as Gijón, with its great stately beach and old port, and Alcoi, with its historic city center built on a gorge surrounded by rugged mountain formations, might seem more likely to attract the visit of tourists than the research of sociologists. Indeed, many locally or regionally specific stories can be told about these towns. Their specificities are undeniable. But there is a thread of shared causality, a logic of social relations, that can be found in the overall set of industrial towns. Moreover, the conceptual rationale for grouping these communities together, the demographic predominance within them of the industrial working class, focuses our empirical research on what has been a collective actor of undeniable political significance in the twentieth century: the most basic lines of political life cannot be traced without including political parties and social actors that claim to represent, and to speak for, the industrial working class. Indeed, it has been argued that Western democracy rests, above all, on the efforts and the political sensibilities of the organized working class.[39] Whether one accepts or rejects that strong claim—and readers of this book will certainly differ among themselves on that question—what is currently unclear is whether the organized working class will continue to play a vital role in charting the course of democratic life during the twenty-first century. Many factors—the numerical decline in the "traditional" industrial working class, the political salience of nonclass identities, changes in the international political economy that may undermine the viability of pro-labor policies, and the crisis and loss of credibility of some among the principal political solutions or strategies (whether social democratic, communist, or otherwise) historically based on the working class—have combined to place in

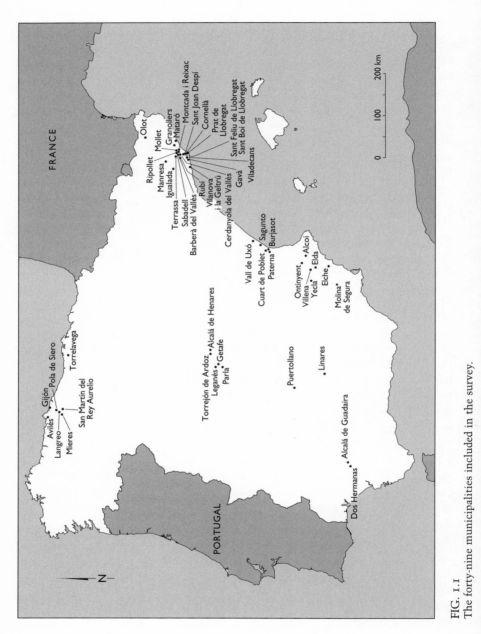

FIG. 1.1
The forty-nine municipalities included in the survey.

question the relative importance of the working class in the shaping of democratic political life. Will workers, their communities, and those who speak in their name significantly help to determine "the quality of democratic life," or will workers stand essentially as politically isolated individuals, irrelevant to the processes at work in the political arena? Will working-class communities generate a public discourse capable of engaging a broad national audience—and thus contribute to the wider public arena's quality—or will their collective endeavors take a form likely to be perceived as "noise" to be filtered out rather than reflected upon? These questions, along with the more broadly posed one about social ties and the quality of democratic life, are addressed by my research on industrial communities.

Subcultures Defined

In exploring the consequences generated by worker–intellectual ties, I have found it useful, indeed essential, to differentiate between those ties organized around (or within) organizations belonging to the socialist tradition and those falling within the communist or post-communist tradition of sociopolitical activism. I refer to these two groupings as *subcultures*. Given the fairly broad set of meanings this term has acquired in social science writing, I consider it useful to elaborate here the sense in which I use the term. As I shall explain, I use the term in a somewhat tighter and more precise way than do those for whom *subculture* refers simply to a group of people sharing a salient demographic characteristic or region of residence and thought likely, on average, to view social life in a manner somewhat distinct from the larger society.[40] New Englanders, young people, chess players, Sicilians, retirees, and so on—in the view I elaborate— may or *may not* constitute subcultures. More than simple shared membership in an identifiable group or setting should be required for us to comfortably speak of a subculture. Yet I also use the term in a somewhat looser sense than do scholars who see subcultures as necessarily *tight* communities of meaning. Thus I find overly demanding, at least for the phenomena here examined, the formulation of noted cultural sociologist Wendy Griswold, for whom a subculture possesses "a powerful set of symbols, meanings, and behavioral norms—often the opposite of those in the larger culture—that are binding on the subculture's members." For Griswold, subcultures entail "a way of life," a standard far more restrictive than that required by the conception of subcultures presented here and surely too restrictive to permit us to conceive of the socialist and post-communist spheres in such terms.[41]

I understand a subculture to exist where a given subset of a larger population organizes its interactions around a set of understandings that are known and shared within the subcultural group and that differ, in at least some meaningful respects, from those found externally. Subcultures in this sense may or may not be geographically contiguous, and they need not close themselves off from the larger societies. The demarcations or boundaries separating subcultures from the broader social world should be relatively clear, but they need not be impervious. Moreover, subcultures themselves, much like the larger cultures within which they are to be found, may well be highly heterogeneous internally so long as participants share an understanding of the range of behaviors and interactions that may be expected and tolerated within the group's boundaries. Subcultures, in this sense, can be characterized by Lyn Spillman's useful formulation of cultures as "repertoires of meanings and values, some of which are heard widely, some of which are less commonly heard."[42] There is scholarly precedent for understanding subcultures to encompass substantial internal differences, and it is useful to elaborate here how our recognition of that heterogeneity can be reconciled with the claim that (some) interactions must still be understood to occur within subcultures.[43]

In this sense, some youth subcultures may see drug use as normal (but not required) behavior; in such a setting, to denounce drug use would be looked down upon. An abstinent young person might belong to this subculture, but only insofar as she or he is comfortable in the near vicinity of standard subcultural behaviors such as drug use. Other young people uncomfortable with drug use might well maintain some friendships with subculture members, but their interactions would have to be located outside the thick subcultural setting, occurring instead in external or individualized venues, be they religious, family-centered, sports-related, or whatever. In the same vein, an intellectually oriented subculture of students may include members with varying commitment to the discussion of ideas, but a student uncomfortable around such interchange would not "fit in."

I use *subculture* in this sense to refer to the spheres of interaction around and within, on the one hand, the Socialist Party (PSOE throughout most of Spain, and PSC-PSOE in Catalonia) and the socialist-oriented union confederation (UGT), and on the other hand, all postcommunist political formations (most importantly the PCE— in Catalonia, PSUC—and the larger umbrella organization Izquierda Unida [IU], and its rough Catalan equivalent Iniciativa per Catalunya [IC], and the historically allied union confederation Comisiones Obreras [CCOO]). I have coded respondents as belonging to a sub-culture if they are affiliated with or represent in some official sense one of its core political or union organizations. With this definition, nearly half the respondents, 150, fall within the postcommunist sub-culture, whereas a slightly smaller number, 125, belong to the social-ist subculture. A smaller number of respondents, 24, belong to neither subculture, and 6 respondents (who have been excluded from the subcultural analysis) hold dual memberships, thus belonging to both subcultures.[44]

All of those belonging to neither sphere, along with many classi-fied within one or the other subculture, entered the sample in its second, "snowball" phase. In the second stage of interviewing, respondents were chosen randomly from the list of suggestions pro-vided by first-stage respondents, leaders selected on institutional grounds.

The socialist and postcommunist subcultures, when defined in this sense, overlap substantially in their ideological underpinnings, and they engage in joint actions from time to time. Nonetheless, the two subcultures differ in the range of understandings, rhetorics, behaviors, and objectives to be found in their midst, and crucially— for our purposes—they differ in the (range of) meanings or expecta-tions placed on worker–intellectual ties. How significant is this difference for our concern with worker–intellectual relations and their consequences for democracy's public life? I address this ques-tion inductively through data collected in forty-nine localities.

Although we will shortly review some basic descriptive material on the socialist and postcommunist "worlds" and on differences between them, I have treated subculture essentially as a "shadow variable." Thus, rather than directly examining and delineating the shared understandings of the two subcultures in an exhaustive fashion, I instead search for the significance they hold by ascer-taining their ability to condition, in different ways, the impact of worker–intellectual ties on democracy's public rhetorics. If the ties produce roughly similar effects in the two cases, we find no evidence for the importance of the subcultures as a variable or set of contexts shaping the meaning of their participants' social ties. However, if we encounter meaningful disparities between the socialist and post-communist worlds in the impact of the worker–intellectual ties that develop within their midst, then through the "shadow" they have cast we have also found evidence that these two sociopolitical worlds are indeed subcultures shaping the interactions that take place within them. As we shall see, the shadow cast by the two subcultures is unmistakably clear.

A more direct and wide-ranging treatment of the two subcultures would have held obvious advantages in that it would have offered additional information on their defining understandings, yet that was not the primary object of this study. We shall directly examine a few significant features of the two subcultures, but in far less detail than a thorough treatment would entail. We instead encounter the extraordinary significance of the subcultures because of the clear (and somewhat unexpected) impact they exert on the causal power of social ties to reshape public rhetorics. The impact—and thus the shadow cast by the subcultures—should become increasingly clear to the reader as the book progresses.

Plan of the Book

I have endeavored to write as concise a book as possible, in a style accessible to a fairly broad readership yet appropriate for the more specialized professional audience of my fellow social scientists, especially those in the fields of sociology and political science. The book has seven chapters. Following this introductory chapter, the second chapter offers a descriptive introduction to the worker–intellectual ties reported by the survey respondents. It offers readers basic background material helpful for understanding the causal analysis of later chapters. The central claim of the book, that ties between workers and intellectuals often shape what I call the "discursive horizons" of local communities, is presented in chapter 3, with the benefit of material from both qualitative and survey interviews. Chapter 4 contrasts the approach I follow with the currently fashionable "social capital" line of work, offering a broad critique of that concept. I devote substantial attention to this issue to avoid any confusion over whether the social ties I emphasize could appropriately be understood to represent "social capital." Chapter 5, the most quantitatively oriented part of the book, takes up and largely rejects alternative explanations for the form taken by democracy's public rhetorics. Chapter 6 asks whether the findings travel beyond the Spanish case or simply reflect specific features of this one national instance. I take up this question by examining empirical differences between the two politically distinct subcultures of Spain's working-class communities. On this basis I present a generalizing argument differentiating between ties-as-brokerage and ties-as-conversation. The conclusion reflects more speculatively on the implications of my analyses for contemporary democratic life and returns to the opening concern over the quality of democratic life. I also examine in the conclusion the degree to which the empirical story presented here should be taken as specific to the relations between intellectuals and workers or as indicative of more broadly shared features of social ties that cross group boundaries.

2 Exploring Social Ties
Bonds between Intellectuals and Workers

Although the term *social tie* is by now a standard tool of contemporary American sociology, connoting an enormous array of social relationships, the specific focus of this volume on the impact of ties between intellectuals and workers has not been a common theme of American empirical sociology.[1] Many social theorists and political thinkers have written on the subject, offering both observations and reflections, but their theoretical speculations or insights have not tended to generate rigorous empirical analysis; the enormous political and symbolic importance of worker–intellectual ties during much of the twentieth century has not been widely reflected in the research of social scientists. Although in subsequent chapters I frequently take the ties here examined to represent, in a broader sense, connections between socially dissimilar groups, in this chapter I examine more specifically the form taken by intellectual–worker ties and the importance placed on them by at least some of those involved in our forty-nine communities. It is important that we take seriously the specificities of our primary intellectual focus on intellectual–worker bonds, but this specific emphasis will allow us to pose the broader theme of ties between socially dissimilar groups, be they intellectuals and workers, or any other similarly disparate collectivities.

The choice of simple two-way or "dyadic" social ties as the basic conceptual and empirical building block for the analysis affords a strong and clear foundation for exploring phenomena and causal relations that many social scientists might prefer to analyze through more elaborate conceptual lenses such as *networks* and *social capital*. That scholars using these concepts have made major contributions is beyond question (although in chap. 4 we will explore serious criticisms of the social capital concept). Nevertheless, the decision to focus here on simple two-way ties reflects the assessment that this approach is the most useful for our social science purposes as well as the most readily accessible to non–social scientists. I share with many network theorists the view that the network concept should be reserved for studies that rigorously delineate the overall set of both direct and indirect social relations within a population—a methodological challenge so demanding that had I adopted it in this study, it would have displaced much of the time available in the interviews for this study's other main theme, and dependent variable, the quality of democratic life.[2] The direct impact of social ties is among the most enduring fundamental questions of sociology; the complex accumulation of both indirect and direct ties in the form of networks is among the most promising themes in sociology, but network phenomena in all their complexity continue to require highly specialized methodologies if they are to be captured fully. Moreover, full network data are not necessary to answer the question posed by this book. Even broader in its recent impact within the fields of political science and sociology has been the concept of social capital, which—following early theoretical formulations by sociologists James Coleman and Pierre Bourdieu—has been suggestively developed by Robert Putnam in his important work on the civic basis for democracy.[3] Some analysts would doubtless subsume the social ties I emphasize here within the broad array of phenomena studied under the conceptual label of social capital. Yet despite the stimulating contributions of "social capital" theorists, and the real empirical significance of phenomena they address, I find it strongly preferable to conceive of the social relations here examined through the simple and direct concept of social ties rather than the more elaborate—and in the worst case, mystifying—concept of social capital. Nonetheless, I explore the utility of the social capital formulation in chapter 4. Thus we focus in this chapter on the tangible empirical basis of the work: ties between working-class leaders and intellectuals.

Bonds between the working-class and left-oriented theorists or intellectuals have been integral to the self-understanding of large sectors of the Left during much of the twentieth century. Throughout Latin Europe, including Spain, these bonds form a vital, if sometimes problematic, strand in the history of both the communist and the socialist wings of the Left. Not only the importance placed in these ties, but also their actual prevalence even in the late twentieth century, would likely surprise most Anglo-Saxon observers and many from within Latin Europe itself. Before exploring the nature of these ties and their impact on political life, let us first establish their actual prevalence, the frequency with which they are to be found.

Basic Traits and Prevalence of the Ties

Among the local working-class leaders interviewed in our survey, more than two-thirds, 69.8% to be exact, maintained some type of direct contact with intellectuals (see fig. 2.1). This simple number underscores how important the phenomenon we examine is for the Spanish Left and more broadly for Spanish society. But this simple descriptive percentage masks major differences in the nature, intensity, and frequency of the contacts. All of the leaders with contacts were asked to specify the nature of their ties or social interactions with intellectuals. In fact, two separate questions were used to elicit this important information. The first of these questions was open-ended; respondents who indicated that they maintained contacts of some form with intellectuals were asked quite simply what those contacts consisted of. The persons interviewed offered numerous responses to this question, thus providing evidence of the wide range of interactions between working-class leaders such as themselves and intellectuals. Many of the responses indicated *institutional* forms of interaction, such as formal consultations with intellectuals on specific matters of union or party strategy; the invited participation of intellectuals in labor-sponsored talks, seminars, or training sessions; the participation of the respondents themselves in intellectual activities in universities or other cultural centers; and shared projects with intellectuals in formal organizations such as political parties. In the extreme case, some institutionally based ties were founded exclusively on joint participation in upper-level organs or representative bodies of a political party. In contrast to these institutional forms of contact and interaction, some of the responses referred in one way or another to friendship ties or other extra-institutional forms of interaction such as discussions over beer or coffee after the end of official union or party business. To facilitate the coding of these responses into reliable categories useful for analysis, we followed up with a semi-structured question intended to further specify the nature of the ties and interactions. On the basis of these items, we initially coded the responses into the five categories reported in figure 2.1. Those who mention only one type of interaction with intellectuals are

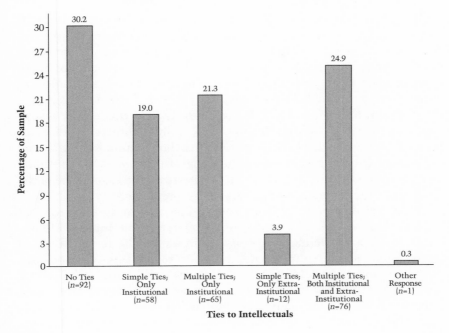

FIG. 2.1
Working-class leaders' ties to intellectuals.

coded as having simple ties; those who report more than one type of interaction—for example, consultations with economic experts, participation in university seminars, and the joint planning of a public lecture series—are coded as having multiple ties.[4] We also coded the responses on the basis of the distinction introduced earlier between institutional and extra-institutional interactions. Thus we begin with the five-category division of the respondents presented in this figure.

In the overall sample of local leaders, fewer than a third, 30.2%, report no contact at all with intellectuals. The next largest group, 24.9%, enjoys multiple contacts with intellectuals, including both institutional and extra-institutional interactions. A slightly smaller segment of the respondents, 21.3%, maintains multiple contacts of an exclusively institutional nature; for this group, interactions with intellectuals are relatively common and varied, but they never take the form of friendship. Somewhat fewer respondents, 19.0%, maintain simple and exclusively institutional ties with intellectuals. A very small segment of the local leaders, 3.9%, maintains simple ties of an exclusively extra-institutional character. Friendship bonds without any basis in current institutional activities are not common, but they do exist, thus linking some local working-class leaders to the world of intellectuals through purely personal interactions. In the analyses in following chapters, I rely largely on a trichotomy distinguishing between leaders lacking ties to intellectuals, those with simple ties, and others with multiple ties, but I retain here the more complete categorization—distinguishing also between institutional and extra-institutional ties—to share with readers a basic sense of the range of experiences found among the respondents.

Who are these intellectuals, tied in one way or another to local working-class leaders? The definition offered in the interview questionnaire clearly delineated the sense in which the term is used in this book, asking respondents to refer to university professors, authors, and artists. Many respondents, whether during the formal survey interview or in separate qualitative interviewing, mentioned specific (often named) individuals who fall clearly into one or another of these categories: university professors of law, sociology, history, and economics; a well-known philosopher; historians and other authors without university affiliations; a novelist; an artist.[5] In some cases respondents were likely referring to individuals on the margins of, or just outside, the definition offered in the interview. It seems probable that when some of those interviewed referred to intellectuals, they were actually thinking of professionals such as practicing lawyers or engineers or in some cases high school teachers. Various comments made during the interviews suggest that on occasion, but not in most instances, respondents may have interpreted the definition offered rather loosely. Suffice it to say that relatively few of the intellectuals connected to workers are individuals of genuinely widespread public renown, most are serious—if less well known—scholars and authors, and a few fall formally just outside the category as I have defined it.

Subcultures as the Contexts of Interaction

As already suggested in the introduction to this chapter, it is useful in our analysis of worker–intellectual ties and the quality of democracy to distinguish between the two principal groupings or "families" of the Spanish Left: the postcommunist subculture, made up of CCOO as well as the various political parties or coalitions originating in the Communist Party, and the socialist subculture, made up of the UGT and the PSOE (in Catalonia the PSC). The large majority of the local leaders interviewed fall into one or the other of these two groupings, although some politically independent leaders and members of other political traditions fall outside of them. This analytical division is clearly rooted in the history and the political identities of the Spanish Left, but following the conceptual guidelines I established earlier in introducing the term, the two groupings I call subcultures are not as compact or self-conscious as would be the case for many collectivities conventionally thought of in those terms. With the exception of a very small number of local contexts, relatively little social and cultural activity is actually organized by the political subcultures, whose activity is instead largely limited to the formal doings and informal discussions surrounding political and labor union affairs. Moreover, organizational divisions and political debates, some of them bitter, separate many of those I place together within one or another subculture. Yet for an understanding of the social ties between workers and intellectuals, the distinction by subculture proves essential. The actual substance of the interactions, their history, and the meaning attached to them vary a good deal between the two cases. And, as I show, the causal impact of the ties is substantially different in the two subcultures. Although I largely treat the subcultures as a "shadow variable" whose features are observed through their effects, rather than by more exhaustive direct observation, it remains useful to touch briefly on a few of the most salient aspects of the two subcultures. We turn, then, to a brief discussion of their histories and politics.

Although it is reasonable to think of socialists and postcommunists as forming somewhat cohesive political communities, they are both highly diverse internally. Much has united, and separated, these two political cousins; during the Second Republic and the Civil War of the 1930s, relations between the two political groupings alternated between periods of cooperation and competition.[6] Also prominent within the Spanish Left of the 1930s was a large anarcho-syndicalist movement, roughly equal in size to the socialists and far larger than the Communist Party until the outbreak of Civil War in 1936. Ideological differences within each of these families of the Left developed in ways significantly more complex than the uninformed observer might assume: the large "maximalist" sector of the Socialist Party, unlike moderate forces within that same party, defended the cause of armed revolution, whereas the Communist Party emphasized the benefits of broad coalitional politics intended to defend the Second Republic from its rightist adversaries. Soviet military support for the republic during the Civil War helped the previously small Communist Party grow quickly after the outbreak of war in 1936, and by the end of the conflict, with the victory of Franco's forces in 1939, the communists had established themselves as a major mass actor.

Franco's repression of labor and the Left was severe, especially in the first years after his victory; as a result, thousands of anti-Francoist Spaniards lost their lives.[7] In the repressive context of the Franco period, the Communist Party came to play a substantially greater role than its socialist counterpart in the organization of oppositional activity; indeed the Communist Party emerged as the central political force of the antiauthoritarian opposition movement. The communists' ability to endure the risks and rigors of clandestine opposition helps explain their success (relative to other left-wing opposition forces), but perhaps equally important was their strategic decision to make use of the limited opportunities for legal activism within the Francoist system, especially within the regime's obligatory "vertical union." The communist-linked labor movement, Comisiones Obreras (CCOO), achieved notable successes in both the institutional strategy of electoral competition within the regime union and the extra-institutional strategy of waging strikes and protests.[8] In the repressive context of the Franco years, Comisiones activists, and others within the communist subculture, shared a series of formative collective experiences: the effort to recruit and mobilize opposition supporters from a wide variety of backgrounds, the risk—or reality—of arrest, and a deep sense of shared identity with fellow activists. This set of experiences was substantially less common outside the communist subculture, although numerous socialist activists, and antiauthoritarian activists of many different political stripes, endured similar circumstances.[9]

This shared experience of political activity under a repressive regime has been as important for the collective identity of the communist subculture in Spain as specific ideological positions, and in fact many subculture participants were attracted to the communists more by their prominence in opposition than their distinctive ideological heritage. Under democracy, many of these veterans of the communist wing of opposition have redefined their identity—some remaining within the subculture, albeit its "postcommunist" component, and others leaving for the socialist subculture or other political homes, including the conservative Partido Popular.

Although virtually any conventional analysis of political tendencies would place the communist subculture to the left of the socialist one, numerous qualifications could be introduced. At more than one point in time, substantial elements within the socialist subculture have adopted positions more militant in nature than their counterparts in the communist subculture. This reversal of the expected pattern of difference occurred at times during the transition to democracy when the Communist Party opted strongly for dialogue, compromise, and moderation to advance the cause of democracy. The socialist labor federation UGT has, at times, taken a more mobilizational approach than its communist subculture counterpart CCOO, most recently in 1998, and in the opinion of some, once again in 2002. Furthermore, the differences of opinion and analysis found within both subcultures provide for a broad area of overlapping perspectives, which is to say that numerous activists could conceivably find themselves at home ideologically in either of the two subcultures. This helps to explain why many political actors have in fact switched from one subculture to the other. This process has usually led from the communist to the socialist sphere of politics, but for some activists the direction of movement has been the reverse. Although it proves useful to think of the two subcultures as communities of interaction, it would not be wise to conceive of them as ideologically homogeneous actors characterized by given political positions. The internal heterogeneity and the political evolution over time have been too great to justify such a view. Indeed, it is for this reason that I refer to the communist subculture by the label *postcommunist*, thus acknowledging the fundamental redefinition of many political actors who remain within that subculture even though they no longer think of themselves as communists.

Before turning to the question of the ties themselves, let us first briefly touch on a bit of direct evidence from the survey on similarities and differences in the fundamental values held by activists in the two subcultures. My purpose here is not to review exhaustively all the politically significant values strongly held by Spanish social-

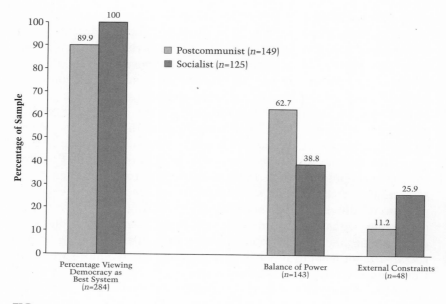

FIG. 2.2
Support for democracy and determinants of success by those seeking change, by subculture. When other subcultures are eliminated from the sample, all relationships
are highly significant; $p < .05$.

ists and postcommunists; my research was not primarily intended to
address that theme. The data presented in figure 2.2 report on
answers to two separate questions, one asking respondents to indicate if they agreed with the assertion that democracy is the best
system for a country such as Spain, and the other asking those interviewed to identify the principal factor determining, in their view, the
success or failure of efforts to change the world through political
action. On the second of these two questions, referred to simply as
"the determinants of political change," I report only those two
answers that manifest a meaningful difference between the two
subcultures.

Democracy as a system elicits overwhelming support from local
leaders in both subcultures. In the sample, that support is unanimous
among leaders from the socialist subculture, whereas a small minority of those in the postcommunist subculture, 10.1% of those inter-

viewed, fails to support democracy. The difference between the two subcultures is minute, yet it reflects the reality that a very small minority in the postcommunist case continued to dream of, or at least contemplate with interest, a Leninist "dictatorship of the proletariat." Nonetheless, this small segment of that subculture should not obscure the fact that even among postcommunists, unambiguous support for democracy is almost uncontested—a pattern that helps explain the success of Spain's post-Franco political transition. Greater differences between the two subcultures appear in their perceptions of the determinants of political change. Postcommunists, who apparently hold a struggle-based vision of politics, are most likely to mention as determinant the balance of power between forces favoring and opposing change. This response is chosen by 62.7% of the postcommunists and 38.8% of the socialists. In contrast, the limitations imposed by external constraints appear far more visible to socialist leaders, among whom 25.9% choose this answer, than to postcommunists, of whom but 11.2% of those interviewed select this reply. This simple disparity ultimately proves telling in making sense out of the causal "shadow" cast by the subcultures. Postcommunists have maintained a culture focused on dedication to struggle and on objectives generally farther left than those pursued by mainstream socialists. Spanish socialists, on the other hand, are more strongly swayed than their postcommunist counterparts by a perception of external constraints that limit social democratic reformers' ability to enact those changes they desire, in principle. We will have cause to return to this fundamental contrast when, in chapter 6, we explore explanations for major differences in the effect of social ties within the two subcultures.

Ties within the Two Subcultures

To what degree do leaders in the two subcultures actually manifest disparate patterns of activity or *contrasting meanings* in their linkages to intellectuals? On the surface, and at the most basic level, the pattern of ties appears remarkably similar in the two subcultures. Although the data in figure 2.1 showed a wide range of variation in local leaders' interactions with intellectuals, virtually none of this basic variation in the nature and intensity of ties can be attributed to systematic differences between the two subcultures. The greatest contrast between the two families of the Left, if we focus on the percentage of local leaders found within any one given category of interaction (among the five categories reported in fig. 2.1), is under 4%.[10] Nevertheless, this initial appearance of similarity between the two subcultures is in some measure misleading, as we shall see when we analyze the actual impact and the substance of the ties.

To facilitate the analysis, I have generated two simple categorizations or codings of the respondents' ties, one focused on the volume of the ties and the other on their nature. I rely most heavily on the first of these categorizations, the basic division of the local leaders into those with no ties, simple ties, and multiple ties. (Respondents who mentioned one type of contact or interaction with intellectuals were coded as having simple ties; those who mentioned two or more types of contact—say, for example, consultation with intellectuals on local strategy and joint participation in an association promoting local development—were coded as having multiple ties.) Second, I categorized the respondents on the basis of the nature of their ties, distinguishing between those whose contacts were exclusively institutional and others whose interactions with intellectuals included extra-institutional ties of friendship, or some other personal interaction—such as long discussions over beer or coffee—outside the scope of official union and party business. This renders a three-way classification into those with no ties, those with exclusively institutional ties, and those with ties including some extra-institutional component that reflects personal interactions outside the framework of official business. Those in the third category, including friendship ties, may or may not also maintain institutional linkages to intellectuals through the official formalized activity of union or party. These categorizations of the respondents simplify the data reported in figure 2.1, rendering two alternate trichotomies.

Intellectuals' Disenchantment with Workers: The Decline of Social Ties in the Two Subcultures

Although the data from my research show that social ties between workers and intellectuals are more prevalent than many observers likely would have expected, it remains the case that the connections between these two social groups have weakened substantially in the late twentieth century. Indeed, the widely shared perception of a growing separation or "divorce" between these two classic pillars of the Latin European Left, workers and intellectuals, helped motivate the empirical work underpinning this book: a basic question in designing the research was how working-class politics—and its contribution to the public debate and liveliness of democracy—would be affected by the decline in intellectual–worker ties.

In the decade of the 1980s, the disenchantment of left-oriented intellectuals with workers and labor helped generate a decrease in social ties between these two groups, a decline in interactions that was carefully documented by Paolo Di Rosa in his study of Spanish intellectuals,[11] and was experienced directly within working-class contexts by many of those I interviewed several years later. In the survey, I asked the local leaders if they believed that the interest of intellectuals in workers and working-class organizations had increased, decreased, or remained about the same during the previous ten years. As the data in figure 2.3 show, a clear majority of those interviewed, 62.4%, believed that the intellectuals' interest in labor had declined during the decade prior to the survey. Roughly one-third as many, 21.1%, offered the opposite opinion, that the intellectuals' interest in labor had actually increased. A somewhat smaller group, 16.5%, held the intermediate view—that there had been no real change in the intellectuals' interest in labor. These data are clear on several points: the disenchantment of many intellectuals with workers and labor has been perceived by a large majority of local leaders in working-class communities, but this perception is far from unanimous. Many local leaders hold exactly the opposite impression, believing that intellectuals have increased their concern for workers.

If we focus on the contrast between socialists and postcommunists, we find a strong difference between the two subcultures. Whereas nearly three-quarters of the postcommunist subculture believes that intellectuals have tended to lose interest in workers, the distribution of opinion is much less one-sided among the socialists: fewer than half of them note a decline in intellectuals' interest, and a substantial minority of the socialist leaders, 35.2%, perceives that intellectuals have actually developed an increasing concern for workers during the 1980s. Only a small minority within the postcommunist subculture, 9.5%, expresses this view, asserting that intellectuals' interest in workers had been increasing. The two subcultures that seemed virtually indistinguishable from one another

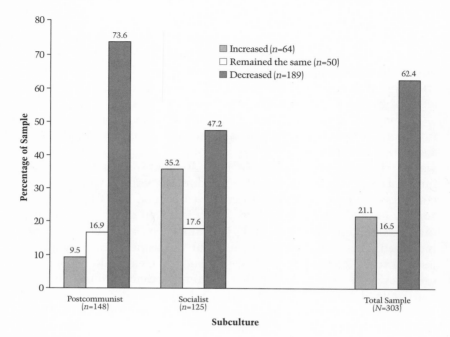

FIG. 2.3
Respondents' perceptions of the evolution of intellectuals' concern for workers and the working class during the 1980s, by subculture. When other subculture answers are eliminated from the sample, the relationship between perceptions of the evolution of intellectuals' concern for workers and subculture is highly significant, at $p = .000$.

when we examined only the simple distribution of ties between local leaders and intellectuals can now be seen as substantially different spheres of social interconnection; these data suggest that the socialist and postcommunist spheres of interaction between intellectuals and workers generate substantially different perceptions—quite likely as a result of meaningful disparities in the nature of those interactions, disparities presumably not captured by the basic categorization of ties I earlier introduced.

The dissimilarities between the two subcultures, both in the actual experiences generated by the social ties and the meaning attributed to them, are multiple in nature and no doubt complex. One simple, and relatively small, difference lies in the historical evolution of the actual contacts maintained by the leaders we interviewed.

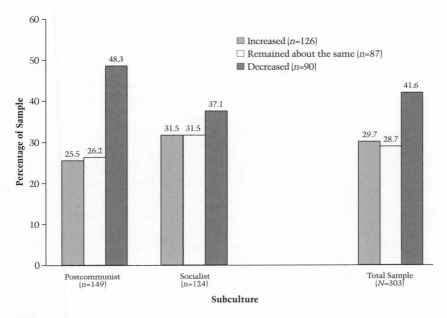

FIG. 2.4
Evolution of leaders' contact with intellectuals during the 1980s. When other
subculture answers are eliminated from the sample and Pearson's chi-square test of
association is used, the relationship does not reach statistical significance ($p = .175$);
when the linear-by-linear test of association is used, $p = .09$.

As the data in figure 2.4 show (in which I report data for the sample
as a whole and for the two subcultures taken separately), a plurality
of the leaders, 41.6%, reported that their ties to intellectuals had
declined either greatly or somewhat during the 1980s. A smaller
group, 29.7%, reported exactly the reverse, that its contacts with
intellectuals had increased to one extent or another during the 1980s.
The two subcultures appear to be relatively distinct from one another
in the prevalence of these opposite experiences. In the postcommunist sphere, the decline in ties to intellectuals has been somewhat
more widely experienced at a personal level than in the socialist
sphere. Whereas 48.3% of the postcommunist leaders reported a
decline in contacts with intellectuals, a smaller proportion of the
socialist leaders, 37.1%, shared the experience of declining ties. On
the other hand, a substantial minority within the socialist subculture, 18.5%, reported increasing ties to intellectuals during the 1970s,

the ten years prior to the survey, whereas within the postcommunist subculture a smaller 10.1% of leaders noted the same positive experience. The contrast in this case is not large in magnitude, but the pattern is meaningful: socialist leaders are more likely than their counterparts in the postcommunist world to have enjoyed an increase in interactions with intellectuals during a period of time in which ties were generally declining. This reverse trend experienced by many socialist respondents reflects, in part, the relatively recent incorporation of some local socialist leaders into active political life—and thus into the circle of working-class elites who might plausibly hope to maintain meaningful contacts with intellectuals—and in part it reflects the passage of some Spanish intellectuals from the postcommunist to the socialist sphere during the 1980s, thus changing the relative balance between the two subcultures in the number of such individuals available for ties to working-class leaders. Thus the contrast between socialists and postcommunists in their perception of the intellectuals' level of interest in workers is matched by a clear disparity in the actual experience of those leaders active in the two subcultures. More significant, however, is the actual content of the interactions, the theme to which we now turn.

How Local Leaders and Intellectuals Experience Their Ties

The actual practices and experiences generated by social ties are, presumably, more decisive than the simple existence—or absence—of those ties in shaping their causal impact on the nature of public life. Numerous stories related by the local leaders included in the qualitative interviews, and by the intellectuals studied earlier by Di Rosa, help provide a sense of the actual fabric of social interaction between intellectuals and workers—an understanding that the more formal survey interviews may not fully capture. Both intellectuals and local working-class leaders vividly remember the ties forged within the opposition movement during the authoritarian Franco period, but they also clearly note a major change in the substance of ties in the post-Franco democratic context. The political passion once placed in intellectual–worker linkages has clearly waned, but for many Spaniards the actual practical substance of such ties has increased, thus yielding a new if less ideologically charged sense of their meaning.

The intellectuals interviewed by Di Rosa offer immensely valuable testimonies of their interactions with labor activists and other workers. A professor of economics in Barcelona relates that in the late Franco period,

> there were frequent relations between workers and intellectuals, and between workers and students. A fluid relationship truly did exist. Clandestine, yes; but it happened in the struggle, on the streets, at demonstrations. The ties were indeed quite strong. I recall that at the time there were sessions aimed at the creation of worker cadres, conferences, interviews with workers by students and the rest of us at the university, and lots of seminars on such issues as the political struggle, on the economy . . . on a thousand different things.[12]

An articulate labor leader in the Nalón valley of Asturias offered a similar perspective in 1994, noting that workers and intellectuals participated jointly in numerous opposition activities during the last decade and a half of Francoism. Moreover, he explained, "the nexus was political. That always happened here."[13] The memory of that politically based nexus remains strong for many of those who experienced it. As sociologist Antonio Izquierdo related to Di Rosa in 1986,

> A large number of the intellectuals who were deeply involved in the labor movement were likewise involved with the universities, and during the Franco period the relation between the labor movement and the student movement was much stronger than it is today; incomparably stronger. In those days the workers would go to the universities when there were strikes to discuss their problems, and many students in turn frequently visited the factories.[14]

A skeptical reader might wonder how meaningful such discussions really were. Apparently some of the participants in those interchanges initially shared that uncertainty, as in the case of Izquierdo himself, who "found it remarkable that factory workers would listen so attentively to a university professor."[15] Nonetheless, this politically charged connection was not to last, at least not in its initial form.

Once democracy was restored in 1977, with the holding of the first free elections in more than forty years, many factors converged to

erode, at least partially, the ideologically oriented political nexus that
had joined workers and intellectuals in the opposition movement. In
this process, the Spanish experience of transition to democracy overlapped historically—and in its causal impact on worker–intellectual
ties—with more widely experienced sociopolitical transformations
that reshaped this, and other, underpinnings of the Left in numerous
European countries. Intellectuals, many of whom had once seen
workers either as a primary vehicle to attain political power or as a
trustworthy ally in the search for paths toward socialism, soon developed more limited and nuanced expectations.[16] Workers, who under
authoritarianism had lacked an autonomous and institutionalized
collective voice, finally gained representation through unions and
parties that often focused, as in any democratic setting, on tangible
and rather limited objectives. This double transformation, of both
intellectuals and workers, weakened the Franco-era political nexus
but opened the door to a new, more practically oriented basis for
worker–intellectual ties. Professor of political philosophy Carlos
París formulated the matter clearly in 1986: "During the dictatorship,
there had been a 'mythification' of the working class among intellectual circles. The labor movement had acquired a magical aura,
particularly among students, intellectuals and professionals." Under
democracy, París noted, intellectual–worker contacts became,
"easier, organized and normalized. . . . This has produced a much less
magical vision of the working class, and a more realistic contact
which is not the daring, adventuresome, forbidden contact maintained during the Franco era."[17]

Although some worker–intellectual interaction under democracy
has continued to focus on large political objectives—whether comprehensive social reforms, a grand project of systemic transformation,
or the mundane pursuit of political power as an end in itself—in some
measure quite practical objectives and concerns have also underpinned the ties. This shift, from the clandestine nexus of shared antiauthoritarian opposition to a new more pragmatic set of connections,
has not been universally possible. Local leaders I interviewed in
Mieres, the largest city in the Caudal mining valley of Asturias,
recalled the existence of significant worker–intellectual interactions
during the opposition period, when "there was permanent contact,"
but underscored the general absence of such ties in more recent years
under democracy.[18] Many localities have shared, to one degree or
another, the massive decline experienced in Mieres. In some such

contexts, intellectual–worker ties became almost nonexistent in the post-Franco period, but in other local settings such connections have remained an important component of sociopolitical life, but with the substance of worker–intellectual interactions often now focusing, at least in part, on specific practical issues. Leaders in Langreo, the largest municipality in the Nalón coal valley of Asturias, remembered as significant their consultations with geography professor (and former Langreo mayor) Aladino Fernández on various urbanistic questions, as well as discussions with other intellectuals on water-use issues and the inclusion of university professors in roundtable debates on ecological topics. These same Nalón leaders lamented that intellectuals would participate in joint activities only if the specific theme to be discussed was of interest to them, perhaps an inevitable frustration in the context of normal democratic politics.[19] Consultations with urbanists and economists have taken place in other industrial towns facing quite different economic challenges. For example, a working-class IU leader in Elda, a small shoe-manufacturing city in Alicante province, identified as important discussions with intellectuals about urban development questions.[20] Core activities of unions, such as negotiations with employers, have also served to channel some interactions. A retired miner in Asturias, himself a rather isolated (and unsuccessful) advocate for building worker–intellectual connections in the Caudal valley where he had been employed, underscored the usefulness of consulting with university professors during collective bargaining processes.[21]

Thus under democracy, in at least some instances, a concrete and practical focus replaced the strongly political and ideological underpinning of worker–intellectual ties that had characterized the late Franco period. This fundamental shift helps explain how the ties I emphasize could remain meaningful and relatively common, despite the crisis and decline of many of those political organizations and movements within which they initially emerged. However, this is not to say that *all* ties came to focus on practical problems or that politics disappeared from the concerns and motivations of workers and intellectuals who found opportunities to interact. Clearly, pragmatic endeavors and political projects were strongly intertwined with one another in many of the activities and interactions related by the respondents. Moreover, in both subcultures, very general political concerns of little immediate practical relevance to the localities studied continued to animate some worker–intellectual interactions.

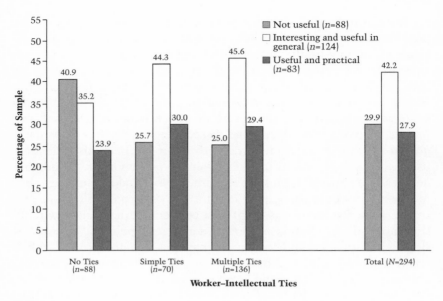

FIG. 2.5
Evaluation of worker–intellectual ties by linkage to intellectuals. The linear-by-linear test of association, appropriate in this instance because of the symmetrical indicators, reaches statistical significance at $p = .05$. However, the ordinal-by-ordinal test reaches marginal significance at $p = .06$.

These qualitative findings are quite suggestive, but they leave us without a complete and full sense of the relative magnitude of differing models of connection.

The formal survey affords helpful and more precise findings on the nature of the interactions and the meanings attributed to them by the interviewed leaders. We asked the respondents to indicate their impression of the usefulness, if any, of contacts with intellectuals. The data reported in figure 2.5 show that a clear majority of the leaders see the ties as useful in one respect or another. The largest group of respondents, 42.2%, considers the ties to be "interesting and also useful even if only with respect to general ideas and orientations." A somewhat smaller segment, 27.9%, contends that the ties are "interesting and also useful for both general and practical matters." Both of these responses are somewhat more common among those with ties than among those without such contacts. The exact mechanism and the direction of causality underpinning that finding cannot be fully resolved at this point, but the fact that those who interact with intellectuals are more likely to view such contacts as useful encourages us to see the ties as meaningful in some sense, as more than empty and formal encounters, thus confirming the view provided by the qualitative material.

The activities and conversations that constitute the actual substance of intellectual–worker ties may vary substantially from one individual case or local setting to another, but a large majority of the leaders finds the ties useful in some fashion. To some degree this belief in the usefulness of the ties appears to reflect actual experiences rather than simple wishful thinking; the leaders linked to intellectuals are those most likely to see the ties in a positive light. This raises the question of whether the ties represent an instrumental strategy on the part of working-class leaders who build social relations with intellectuals as a way of attaining some desired and preconceived objective(s). Many social science analysts would be inclined to see the ties in this consciously instrumental light. Our data on the respondents' perception of the contacts' actual utility make it possible to carefully examine that question when, in chapters 4 and 5, we assess explanatory strategies that differ from the book's central argument. Suffice it to say, for now, that worker–intellectual ties may also develop as a by-product of routine social life in some settings, and in other cases they may be constructed for their perceived intrinsic worth. The ties may or may not reflect instrumental strategies.

Crucial to our understanding of intellectual–worker ties is whether their perceived utility is roughly equivalent or fundamentally different in the two subcultures. We address this question by comparing the perceptions of socialist and postcommunist leaders (see fig. 2.6). As the data show, the postcommunist leaders are substantially more likely than their counterparts in the socialist subculture to view the ties as useful in practical matters. In the postcommunist sphere, roughly one-third of the respondents, 33.8%, choose the most favorable of the alternatives offered them in the interview, the view that contacts with intellectuals are "interesting and also useful for both general and practical matters." This strongly positive evaluation of the ties, emphasizing their practical and general utility, is less widely shared in the socialist subculture, where 20.5% of the respondents choose this alternative. These quantitative findings underscore the importance of actual practical discussions

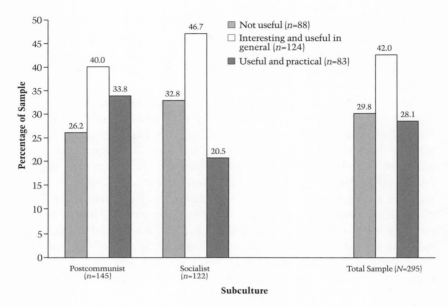

FIG. 2.6
Evaluation of worker–intellectual ties by subculture. When other subculture answers are eliminated from the sample, the relationship is significant at the $p = .05$ level or better.

and advice in the interactions between postcommunist-sphere intellectuals and leaders, an interpretation strongly confirmed in numerous qualitative interviews. Suggestions from labor lawyers on strategies for collective bargaining, discussions with engineers on re-industrialization, interchanges with economists or urbanists on local development strategies and the contribution of historians to elabo-rating public manifestos—all of these activities mentioned by local leaders in one or another of our forty-nine communities fall within the repertoire of experiences shared by local working-class leaders in the postcommunist subculture. This is not to say that practical problem solving and concrete programmatic initiatives fully displace broad overarching political discussions in this subculture. Far from it. The survey responses of the leaders and the stories they relate emphasize the role of both general ideas and specific practical matters in their discussions with intellectuals. But the fact that general polit-ical or theoretical reflections are often accompanied by practically oriented discussions may help explain the findings in chapter 3 showing the strong impact of ties on political discourse within this subculture.

Practical matters, to be sure, are not fully absent from the interactions between socialist intellectuals and local leaders. A substantial proportion of the socialist leaders—albeit many fewer than in the postcommunist subculture—indicate their sense that contacts with intellectuals are "interesting and also useful for both general and practical matters." Local leaders within the socialist sphere also maintain concrete discussions with intellectuals about programs and strategies. However, the culture of interaction has clearly been somewhat different in these two politically differentiated worlds. The presence of the Socialist Party in government from 1982 until 1996, a theme to which we will return in chapter 6, may well stand as one of the most powerful factors in explaining this difference. For many socialist-oriented intellectuals during this period, the great focus of their political energies, enthusiasm, and networking was the center of political power in Madrid. Brief trips to industrial towns such as the forty-nine localities I have studied might find space on the crowded calendar of a socialist intellectual, but if the purpose of such a trip was to deliver a talk on Spain's role in the new Europe or on the welfare state in comparative perspective, little time might be allotted for concrete discussion of the specific challenges faced by the community in which the lecture was delivered. The responsibilities and aspirations generated by national political power left less time for such practically oriented local discussions than many socialist intellectuals might have otherwise wished.

One additional explanatory factor deserves mention. In the closing years of the twentieth century, the political concerns of numerous communist-oriented intellectuals remained focused, at least in part, on the classic working class, whereas the center of gravity in the political mind-set of many socialist-oriented intellectuals had shifted toward other actors and problems. In the same historical context, many left-oriented intellectuals have refocused the center of their own political activity from the postcommunist to the socialist subculture, a shift in allegiance that reduces the pool of authors and academics available for interactions with postcommunist working-class leaders, thus helping to explain their deceasing connection to intellectuals. Pilar Brabo, a prominent communist-turned-socialist, explained in 1986 her (quite characteristic) thinking on the declining relevance of the classic working class: "Already a majority of people in Spain work in the service sector rather than the industrial one. Given these circumstances it is not remarkable that the role of industrial factory workers as main protagonists of the Left is in decline. The socialist project simply adapts to that reality."[22] In contrast, the continued emphasis within the postcommunist subculture on the problems and roles of industrial and manual workers encourages intellectuals in that political sphere to dedicate substantial energies to concrete issues and problems confronting their working-class allies. The declining pool of postcommunist intellectuals has been more fully engaged with its working-class contacts than has its larger socialist subculture counterpart.

Thus, *some* of the difference between socialists and postcommunists in the culture of worker–intellectual interaction may be attributable to the mind-set and agenda of the intellectuals themselves. It would, however, be highly questionable and inconsistent with my research findings to place the predominant weight of explanation exclusively with the intellectuals as a social group. We can also identify clear differences in the practices and attitudes of socialist-oriented versus communist-oriented working-class leaders, differences that help explain contrasts between the two subcultures. But more importantly, there is no reason to assume that subcultural variation should be attributed to workers or intellectuals taken in isolation; the ties here studied by definition involve interactive relations between the two groups.

Locating the Responsibility for the Emergence (and Decline) of Ties

It proves useful to examine the local leaders' response to a question posed in the survey asking them to place with intellectuals or with workers the primary initiative in establishing ties between the two groups. The leaders are far from unanimous in their assessment, as the data in figure 2.7 show, but they are clearly more likely to grant labor than intellectuals the credit for initiating the ties; those placing the initiative primarily with labor are more than double the number of those placing the initiative primarily with intellectuals. It is striking that the leaders maintaining multiple ties to intellectuals are those most likely to place the initiative with labor rather than intel-

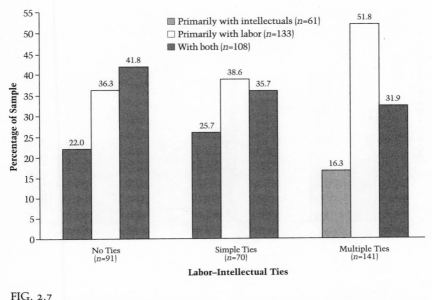

FIG. 2.7
Perceived location of initiative in forming labor–intellectual ties by respondents' ties.
Pearson's chi-square statistical test of association nears significance at $p = .12$.

lectuals. In this most heavily connected segment of the local labor
leadership, 51.8% place the initiative mostly with labor. The perceptions expressed by the local leaders are presumably subject to
some unavoidable bias if only because these working-class leaders are
inevitably aware of their own initiative and possibly unaware of the
initiative supplied by some intellectuals. Yet despite the obvious sub-
jectivity of the leaders' responses here examined, their placement of
the initiative for the ties proves highly suggestive; although their perceptions are an inadequate reflection of reality, they do reflect the
efforts the leaders are aware of having made, and thus their responses
prove telling in my analysis of differences between segments of the
local leadership. The data clearly suggest that the multiple ties maintained by nearly half of the respondents are often constructed by the
local leaders through substantial effort and initiative; the contacts are
typically not an automatic result of the institutionally defined position of the leaders.

It is crucial to note that the working-class leaders cannot simply
will into existence any social ties they might wish to maintain. The

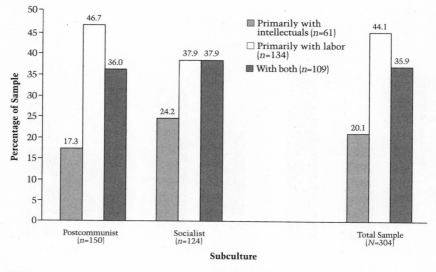

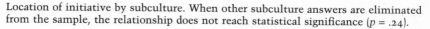

FIG. 2.8
Location of initiative by subculture. When other subculture answers are eliminated from the sample, the relationship does not reach statistical significance ($p = .24$).

ties quite obviously require a minimally favorable social climate on both sides—at least some favorable predisposition on the part of the workers and the intellectuals involved. But if multiple ties are to be formed on the basis of this favorable climate, effort is typically required, and the data suggest that, at least in the perception of the leaders interviewed, that effort has tended to fall disproportionately on the side of the working-class leaders.[23] This introduces an obvious question: To what degree are the local leaders of the two subcultures equally inclined to exert the effort (normally) required to build and maintain contacts with intellectuals?

The socialist and communist subcultures appear somewhat different in their sense of the relative contribution of workers and intellectuals to the ties, as the findings reported in figure 2.8 show. The postcommunist leaders are more inclined than their socialist counterparts to locate the primary initiative for the ties within the circle of labor itself. Nearly half of the postcommunist leaders, 46.7%, and a smaller proportion of the socialists, 37.9%, see labor as disproportionately responsible for the contacts. Perhaps more telling than this simple comparison of the overall pool of leaders in the two subcultures is the contrast one can draw between the two cases *within* the segment maintaining multiple ties. For these most heavily interconnected leaders, the disparity between the two spheres is rather marked. More than half the postcommunist leaders, 54.9%, locate the initiative primarily with labor, whereas many fewer socialist leaders, 40.0%, respond in a similar fashion.[24] Granted, these differences do not represent a contrast so sharp as that of day and night, but they do suggest a disparity between the two subcultures in the effort labor leaders typically consider necessary to maintain contacts with intellectuals. Postcommunist subculture leaders who are highly connected to intellectuals are more likely than their social-ist subculture counterparts to stress their own contribution to gen-erating ties with intellectuals. From this finding I draw a simple inference: that the working-class leaders of the postcommunist sub-culture are more inclined than socialist leaders to see themselves as heavily committed to their interactions with intellectuals. To put this another way, within the working-class component of the post-communist subculture, ties to intellectuals, and the effort normally required to sustain them, are on average somewhat more highly valued than they are in the working-class sector of the socialist subculture.

Thus we cannot attribute all differences between the socialist and postcommunist spheres of labor–intellectual interaction to a pre-sumed lesser commitment of the socialist intellectuals to the practical concerns of workers. Within the working-class component of the postcommunist subculture, the greater conviction of the ties' actual utility is coupled with a heightened sensitivity toward the efforts involved in building the interactions. One is tempted to search for causal order in this constellation, but it is not easy to ascertain one. What we have ascertained is, nonetheless, quite important: that the postcommunist subculture seems a somewhat more fertile ground for meaningful intellectual–worker interactions than is the socialist subculture; that the communist-oriented leaders are more inclined to find practical utility in the ties; that the post-communist-sphere leaders are more likely to see themselves as responsible for building the interactions; that many postcommunist subculture intellectuals value the interactions more strongly than do their socialist counterparts; and that in many settings, postcom-munist intellectuals are now engaged in practically grounded interactions with workers, and focused on concrete issues and challenges.

Whether we focus on intellectuals, on working-class leaders, or on the relations between the two groups, we find substantial variation between the two subcultures in the understandings, expectations, and values that constitute the culture of interaction. No matter what one makes of the ideologies characteristic of these two spheres—or of the policy prescriptions defended through their discourse—it is clear that in the postcommunist subculture, interactions between intellectuals and workers are relatively highly valued. This positive evaluation does not appear to be a simple case of ideologically oriented window dressing; both the effort required to build the ties and the belief in their practical utility are stressed by many communist-oriented local leaders. Thus, if the ties are indeed capable of shaping political life and public discourse, the effect may well be strongest in the subculture that invests the greater effort—and set of expectations—in the ties. The understandings and expectations underpinning the ties have been markedly more robust in the postcommunist subculture than among contemporary Spanish socialists, many of whom fixed their eyes and strategies largely on their party's government in Madrid rather than on locally based social ties.

It is perhaps ironic that the subculture most invested in the interconnections between intellectuals and workers is also the one in which those ties have been most subject to erosion and decline. This withering of ties between workers and intellectuals in the postcommunist subculture might appear to challenge the interpretation here advanced: if those active in the postcommunist subculture genuinely value these ties, why is the decline in ties more pronounced in their midst than in the subculture of their socialist counterparts? This apparent paradox is easily explained by the shift in allegiance on the part of many previously communist-oriented intellectuals throughout the post-Franco period. The decline in ties between intellectuals and workers should not be seen, in any sense, as a phenomenon internal to either of the two cultures but rather as a general trend in the pattern of social relations and the climate of opinion characteristic of Spanish society (and many other national societies as well) in the late twentieth century. But if the trend is indeed a general one, what helps to explain it? A transformation in the perspective of intellectuals, of workers, or of both?

The Withering of Connections between Intellectuals and Labor

The survey data I have collected offer some contribution to our understanding of why and how the contacts between these two groups have tended to wither in recent decades, but a full exploration of this theme would require us to draw on a wider array of material and sources. Surely, broadly macropolitical processes play a contributing role. Thus, for instance, it has been argued that the salience of electronic communication at the time when Spain's democracy was consolidated helped to generate a style of political life low on organization and direct contact. In any event, much can be learned from our research findings. The survey asked a simple question concerning the assignment of responsibility for the deterioration of ties between intellectuals and labor. As the data in figure 2.9 show, a majority of the respondents, 55.5%, place responsibility with both collective actors—intellectuals and workers. Among the respondents who were inclined to emphasize the responsibility of either one or

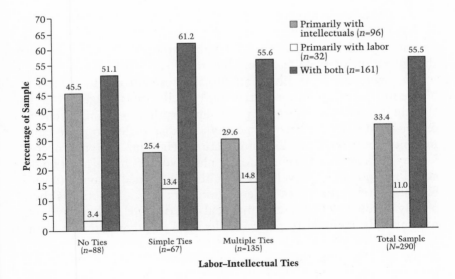

FIG. 2.9
Placement of blame for deterioration of labor–intellectual ties by linkage to intellectuals. Pearson's chi-square test of statistical significance reveals that the relationship is highly significant at $p = .01$.

the other of these two collective actors, substantially more placed the blame primarily on intellectuals, with roughly one-third, 33.4%, holding that view, whereas a much smaller segment of the respondents, 11%, believed labor to be primarily responsible for the decline in ties. This raises the question of whether direct experience on the part of the local leaders has led to the judgment by one-third of those interviewed that intellectuals are primarily responsible for the withering of contacts. A clear pattern can be seen in the data: leaders without ties to intellectuals are those most likely to blame intellectuals for the deterioration of ties. Some of these respondents lacking ties to intellectuals have indeed suffered the direct consequences of waning interest among intellectuals in the working class. When intellectuals lose interest in workers, that loss of interest clearly limits the opportunities for social interconnections between the two groups. But this asymmetry in the placement of blame also reflects a lack of actual experience interacting with intellectuals within the no-ties segment of the respondent pool, thus making it impossible for these leaders to develop a balanced assessment of intellectual–worker relations.

An interesting contrast in the data also merits our attention. The leaders enjoying multiple ties to intellectuals were those most likely to place with labor, rather than with the intellectuals, the credit for the initiation of ties. The fact that those same highly connected leaders were the least likely among the respondents to place the blame for the deterioration of ties with intellectuals suggests clearly that their responses reflect their actual perceptions—be they accurate or not—and have not been shaped by a predisposition to place labor in a more positive light than intellectuals. Had these interconnected leaders been disposed to consistently place workers in the most favorable light possible, they likely would have leaned heavily toward blaming intellectuals for the deterioration of ties, a hypothesis thoroughly rejected by our actual empirical observation. And if they were romantically inclined to place intellectuals in a consistently favorable light, they would likely have offered them disproportionate credit for initiating the ties—again, just the reverse of the actual research observation. Thus we must conclude that the leaders' responses have been relatively uncolored by a predisposition to place either workers or intellectuals within a consistently more favorable light. This does not mean that the leaders' responses can be taken as a fully accurate reflection of reality but simply that their responses reflect their actual perceptions and not an invented image of worker–intellectual relations designed to place one or the other group in a light more favorable than what they have perceived. Thus, on balance, the leaders interviewed offer us their best sense of reality as they see it, affording considerable encouragement to those who believe that survey research, such as that examined here, can provide social scientists, and other readers, an extraordinary opportunity to observe, and causally dissect, the world in which we live.

The Ties as Conversations

We have reviewed many specific questions and empirical findings on the ties between intellectuals and workers, but more than one reader may still be left asking the simple but perfectly reasonable question, So what? The most compelling argument for the importance of social ties between dissimilar social groups such as intellectuals and workers rests squarely on their causal impact, their ability to actually reshape political behaviors—a theme we will explore in detail in the following chapters. But what is there in the actual substance of the ties that generates this substantial causal impact? Perhaps, one line of argument might propose, the ties serve as a conduit of information or ideas. This interpretation fits well the image of group relations and organizational behavior held by many observers. It is not, however, consistent with the empirical findings of this study. Both the survey data and the qualitative interviews lead us to search elsewhere in explaining the ties' impact. As we shall see in the next chapter, the ties do not produce any specific ideological orientation; their causal impact on politics is not reducible to the transmission of any given set of ideas. Information and ideas are transmitted through many vehicles, not only social ties and certainly not only through ties between dissimilar groups such as those here examined.

A thoughtful local leader I interviewed several times in the industrial suburbs of Barcelona suggested a very different way of conceiving the causal impact of the ties. This former secretary general of CCOO in the Baix Llobregat district distinguished between two types of intellectuals, those who interacted with workers as equals and others who came to teach or "explain" their knowledge. He elaborated further that the first type of intellectual listened during interchanges with workers, while the second type seemed only interested in talking. The former secretary general then added, "In the Baix we have been able to absorb the first type and maintain distance with respect to the second."[25] After offering examples of each type, this local leader insisted that the intellectuals who most strongly influenced working-class leaders were those who knew how to *listen*—as well as how to talk. Those intellectuals interested only in communicating a set point of view, he explained, made little impact on the working-class leaders with whom they interacted. I raised this thought with several other local leaders in the final phase of the qualitative interviewing, and their response, without exception, was to smile in agreement. The ties to intellectuals were compelling in so far as they took the form of *conversation*. Where conversations took place, they transformed, in some respects, their participants.

Conversations, by their very nature, require one to *listen* as well as to *speak*, and thus they bring their participants to take cognizance of their conversational partners—of those with whom they wish to interact. Moreover, if conversations are to last, the partners to them must learn how to communicate their thoughts in terms meaningful to other participants. This challenge assumes special importance when the partners in conversation come from substantially different social worlds, as in the case of the workers and intellectuals we examine. The discursive abilities developed in genuine conversations are quite possibly the most important *political* consequence of social ties. Conversations between intellectuals and workers—or between individuals in other dissimilar social groups—carry the ability to reconfigure the sound and tone of political life in arenas far broader than the initial context in which they emerge; such conversations often have the potential to reshape the character of public political discussion and debate.

3 Social Ties and Discursive Horizons

As we shall see in this chapter, social ties powerfully shape the quality of democratic life through their impact on what I shall call discursive horizons, that is, the actual geographic points of reference to be found in public rhetoric—or to put it slightly differently, through the tangible physical location of the problems and proposed remedies discussed by political actors. The term *discursive horizons* may strike some as abstract or even confusing, but it deals with a very real and important aspect of public life: Should the political energies of citizens and indeed of entire towns focus on the defense of specific local interests—jobs, school development, construction projects, and so on—or should they address more widely experienced problems and processes that transcend locality? This question is confronted by local political actors when they formulate objectives and when they adopt a language to communicate and defend those objectives. Discursive horizons—and thus the rhetorical reach of political leaders and activists—take very different forms in the towns we examine. As we shall see, it is precisely these discursive horizons, rather than radicalism, moderation, or any of the other outcomes conventionally analyzed in working-class studies, that are powerfully shaped (in some subcultural contexts) by the social ties of leaders.

The collective energies of Spanish workers and industrial towns are considerable, whether they find expression in strikes and public protest or in more institutionally oriented forms of pressure. The front pages of newspapers and the major stories of television newscasts often relate incidents of worker protest, and this in an age widely thought to be "postindustrial" and to have bid farewell to the working class. Yet these popular energies, and the attention sometimes focused on them, offer no guarantee that public life will be enriched or that democracy will be rendered more vital through workers' political efforts. For most ordinary citizens, do labor's protests and political initiatives represent disruption, inconvenience, and sheer noise to be blocked out to the extent possible, or do labor's endeavors actually engage their attention and offer themes generative of political debate, analysis, and reflection? The answer to this question depends to a great extent on an aspect of politics perhaps less obvious in its importance than conventional objects of study such as the specific content of demands or the identity of protesters; the ability of politics to engage its would-be audience depends greatly on the discursive horizons adopted by the actors.

Despite the enormous variety in the activities and collective efforts launched by labor, it proves extremely useful to draw a rather simple distinction between two highly dissimilar styles of protest and political initiative found in the forty-nine towns surveyed. These contrasting political styles are organized around two fundamentally different sets of discursive horizons: *defensive localism*, to borrow a term formulated by Margaret Weir in her excellent work on American urban politics, clearly characterizes the spirit and style of numerous collective efforts carried out by—or in the name of—workers.[1] The attempt to keep open specific mines slated for closure, to protect existing jobs in money-losing factories, or to maintain a school or clinic in one neighborhood rather than moving it to another—all of these objectives fit easily within the broad political style of defensive localism. The protest banners to be found hanging on numerous Spanish factories where layoffs have been announced and the not-infrequent newspaper headlines telling of confrontations between the police and workers near installations slated for closure attest to the great prevalence, and the public visibility, of defensive localism in Spanish labor politics. But another prevalent and very different style of labor initiative is best defined by its constant search for connections between the local and national (or international) arenas, between specific sources of discontent and general processes that underpin them. Numerous leaders and towns are characterized by this generalizing discourse, by a complex and globalizing rhetoric. The effort to connect the specific to the general, the concrete to the abstract, and the local to the extralocal shapes this discourse. (Of course, other forms of rhetoric are also possible, including the highly abstract or ideological appeal to generalities—largely or completely disconnected from local realities. Nonetheless, I find it useful to emphasize the clear distinction between defensive localism and global discursive horizons.)

The distinction between these two disparate styles of labor politics is quite real, but it is not the sort of thing that tends to be noticed
or commented on by students of politics or even by thoughtful
observers. It was only after analyzing the survey results and carrying
out the subsequent qualitative interviews that the strong lines and
full import of this distinction became clear to me. But rather than
asking the reader to retrace point by point and in sequence all the
steps I have taken as a researcher, I prefer instead to sketch out the
difference between the two styles—or voices—of labor as clearly as
possible before introducing the empirical findings that can help
account for this difference. Perhaps the most widely publicized and
persistent recent case of defensive localism among our forty-nine
communities was the long battle of Linares, in the Andalusian
province of Jaen, to save all the industrial jobs at Santana Motor,
its money-losing automobile factory.[2] In the winter of 1994, the
Japanese firm Suzuki, owners of the Santana factory, announced plans
to radically reduce employment in the Linares plant to help correct
a financial deficit. The Santana workers, strongly supported by the
residents of Linares, responded quickly with a militant campaign
designed to save all twenty-four hundred jobs. Tens of thousands of
Spaniards were directly touched in one way or another by that campaign. The workers marched, demonstrated, struck, blocked major
highways and rail lines, sat in at government buildings, and ultimately marched on both Madrid and Seville to promote their cause
and to spread their acts of disruption beyond the province of Jaen.
The protesters frequently denounced both Suzuki and the government, but the central demand and slogan of their campaign was
unambiguous in its focus: "2,400 Jobs. Not one less!" During the
Holy Week vacation period of 1994, the Santana workers carried out
one of their most poignant and least disruptive actions: a large group
of protesters formed a human chain alongside the major north–south
highway that provides motorists from Madrid and north-central
Spain access to Andalusia. The human chain spelled out a simple
slogan intended to remind vacationers of what the workers believed
to be at stake in their struggle: "Linares," the name of their town,
was the message the protesters conveyed. The sustained expression
of working-class militancy by the Santana protesters was designed to
attract the attention of the national public, but the proclaimed objective of the workers could not have been more local—the defense of
twenty-four hundred good industrial jobs in the town of Linares.

The voice of the Santana workers finds its echo, or antecedent, in numerous other industrial communities. Among the clearest examples is that of the Caudal valley in the Asturian coalfields of northern Spain. At the onset of the 1990s, approximately 10,000 miners continued to work in the unprofitable state-owned coalmines of the Caudal, a valley whose total population in 1990 was just over 100,000. The almost exclusive employer of the miners, the state-owned firm HUNOSA, planned a major program of mine closures for the early part of the decade. The Caudal responded with a militant series of actions: mine occupations, strikes, and demonstrations. The Barredo pit in Mieres, the Santa Bárbara mine in Turón—these and others were the focus of protesters' demands to keep the mines open so as to save jobs. A simple banner placed on Turón's Santa Bárbara mine in 1994 conveyed clearly the spirit of the Caudal's struggles: "For our future. Keep it open." These defensive localistic mobilizations absorbed the energies and expressed the sentiments of valley residents, but they did not succeed in halting the mine closures or in changing the overall political and economic climate that engendered such endeavors.

Some readers might be inclined to suspect that there is something "natural," or in any event predictable, about the Caudal strategy, but only a few kilometers away the response of miners and their communities to the same set of conditions was markedly different. On the other side of a mountain ridge, and separated by twelve kilometers of highway, lies another mining valley, the Nalón, with a total population and an economic panorama remarkably similar to that of the Caudal. The Nalón is in no sense less militant than the Caudal. The pictures displayed in the valley headquarters of Comisiones Obreras in La Felguera de Langreo proudly relate the story of confrontations with police in the course of numerous demonstrations and strikes.[3] But the workers and residents of the Nalón have focused their efforts on far broader and more inclusive objectives, not on the defense of particular mines or specific towns, and again, a simple banner conveyed the essence of the valley's political style. In 1990, motorists entering the valley's second largest municipality, San Martín del Rey Aurelio, were greeted by a slogan hanging above the main highway just inside the city limits: "We demand the reindustrialization of the entire area." The decision of Nalón leaders and protesters to demand, above all, reindustrialization has allowed them not to focus on particular groups of workers or specific mines but instead to appeal to the shared interests of all valley residents and indeed of the entire region of Asturias. Without losing sight of the problems and specificities of the towns within the valley, Nalón leaders have used the demand for reindustrialization to enter extralocal debates over national economic policy, international processes, and regional development. One may agree or disagree with the analysis and proposals articulated in the Nalón, but their relevance to a broad public audience is undeniable. For those who live outside the two valleys, the voice of the Caudal may elicit sympathy, indifference, or even annoyance; in contrast, the voice of the Nalón, and of other locales with similar discursive horizons, may engender reflection, agreement or disagreement, and ultimately response. The Caudal's defensive localism attempts to mobilize residents on behalf of specific small groups found within the valley's confines; the Nalón's globalizing discourse attempts to offer solutions to problems found throughout the valley and well beyond.

Both Asturian mining valleys are firmly militant in their tactics, which is one reason why on occasion they have collaborated in joint efforts (such as the general strike of March 23, 1993). Thus a conventional analyst could easily find common threads in the political and union history of the two valleys. Indeed, miners and their communities stand out not only in the Spanish context but in crossnational studies as well, on the basis of their shared militancy and political commitments.[4] Yet underneath the surface, characterized by conventional markers of militancy, we clearly find in the Asturian coal valleys a strong contrast in emphasis between the globalizing discourse of the Nalón and the tendency toward defensive localism in the Caudal. Moreover, this distinction between defensive localism and generalizing discourse is to be found in communities at widely diverging points on the continuum running from moderation to radicalism and in communities spanning a wide range of industrial profiles. In the far less conflictual textile towns of the Valencian region, a similar contrast can be drawn between generalizing Alcoi and localist Ontinyent, two towns separated by the Mariola mountain ridge and twenty kilometers of highway. And in the frequently pragmatic and economically dynamic working-class suburbs of Barcelona, the moderate unionists of the Baix Llobregat stand as another clear example of generalizers—in contrast to others nearby. Discursive horizons vary enormously among Spanish industrial communities, and this variation appears to follow a logic highly independent of the conventional yardstick that distinguishes among levels of radicalism or moderation. Before exploring in greater detail the actual substance, in political life, of the difference between these two voices of labor, let us first turn to the causal question: What, then, accounts for this difference, and how is it linked to the pattern of social ties at the community level?

Intellectual–Worker Ties and Discursive Horizons

The survey data from local leaders in industrial communities clearly show a relationship between social ties and discursive horizons: Where intellectual–worker ties are prevalent, the probability increases that discursive horizons will be relatively expansive—or, to use the term I prefer, globalizing—routinely emphasizing the *connections* between local problems and broader, more general phenomena; where such ties are weak or absent, this generalizing spirit and thus global discursive horizons are markedly less prevalent. Without these social ties, political life suffers. Narrowly focused proposals and the defense of particular local interests take precedence over the effort to relate locally experienced problems to broad national and international concerns. This difference in discourse must not be seen as an opposition between concrete or local concerns on the one hand and abstract or exclusively extralocal concerns on the other. The globalizing rhetorics of socially connected actors emphasize both local and extralocal phenomena, both concrete and abstract expressions of their concerns. The globalizers, sociologically characterized by social linkages, articulate through their public statements connections among places and problems. These connections in rhetoric and proposals between local and extralocal problems, between specific and general interests, are what mark the distinctive character of the "global discursive horizons."

In the survey-based analysis that follows, I rely heavily on a question about injustice that proves especially helpful in locating and explaining distinctive patterns in the discursive horizons of the local leaders. Those interviewed were asked which among four alternative strategies offered the best political response to the problem of injustice: (1) to identify and discuss specific cases of injustice, (2) to raise the general theme of injustice and the importance of eliminating it, (3) to discuss both concrete cases and the general problem of injustice, or (4) to propose concrete measures to improve life without devoting much time to the discussion of injustice. The third response—emphasizing the juxtaposition of both concrete cases and the general problem of injustice—clearly stands as a strong example of the search for connections underpinning the globalizing discursive horizons we identify as crucially important. In the interests of clarity and simplicity, I have dichotomized the answers to this question, distinguishing between the globalizers—that is, those predisposed to draw connections between the local and the extralocal, the concrete and the abstract, the specific and the general—and all the others. This dichotomization is above all an analytical convenience that sharpens our ability to see causal patterns, but it also makes good substantive sense: among the response categories we have grouped together as the "negative case," the first and fourth responses both emphasize the concrete and the specific to the exclusion of the general; the second response emphasizes the general or abstract to the exclusion of the concrete. In all three instances, generalities and grounded specificities are seen as separate from one another, and thus are not connected. In contrast, the third response reflects a commitment to articulating the connection between specific cases and the general phenomenon of injustice; only this commitment to articulate connections allows one to raise broad extralocal issues and speak to widely felt problems while standing in defense of specific local interests.

As the data in figure 3.1 show, the local leaders with ties to intellectuals are substantially more likely than their counterparts without such ties to choose the third response, showing a predisposition toward global discursive horizons. Moreover, the magnitude of this effect increases somewhat with the strength of the contacts: the drawing of connections between specific and general dimensions of injustice is chosen by 31.1% of local leaders without ties to intellectuals, by 44.1% of those with simple ties to intellectuals, and by 48.2% of those with multiple ties to intellectuals. This first quantitative approximation at the relationship between social ties and discursive horizons establishes a clear although not overpowering association between the two phenomena: the chi-square test showing the quantitative relationship to be statistically significant at the .035 level suggests that we can be reasonably certain that we have encountered a real association between two discrete phenomena, but this initial finding is hardly sufficient on its own to recast our under-

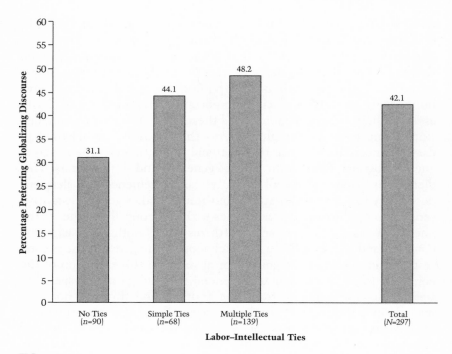

FIG. 3.1
Globalizing discursive horizons by leaders' ties to intellectuals. When the relationship between these variables is tested, Pearson's chi-square test of association reveals a highly significant relationship at $p = .035$; the linear-by-linear test of association reveals $p = .012$.

standing of the linkage between social ties and the quality of democratic life. Yet as we shall soon see in our examination of the survey data and our consideration of various local experiences, the underlying relationship between social ties and discursive horizons is actually far stronger and more meaningful than figure 3.1 suggests—under *certain* conditions.

Specifying the Content of Globalizing Discursive Horizons

Before we proceed further, it will be useful to briefly examine additional survey-based evidence on the role played by both local and extralocal themes in the globalizing discursive horizons found in

TABLE 3.1
Themes of local political debate by ties to intellectuals

Themes of Debate	No Ties (%)	Simple Ties (%)	Multiple Ties (%)	Total (%)	Pearson's Chi-Square
National economic or social policy	21.7	24.3	36.9	29.4	.026**
National political debates and campaigns	7.6	11.4	12.8	10.9	.460
Ideological and general programmatic discussions	8.7	8.6	4.3	6.6	.308
Local economic problems and initiatives	23.9	14.3	32.6	25.7	.015**
Local social problems	16.3	8.6	28.4	20.1	.002***
Local politics	7.6	15.7	15.6	13.2	.165
International and/or war and peace	15.2	5.7	14.9	12.9	.125
N	92	70	141	303	

$*p < .10$ $**p < .05$ $***p < .01$

some but not all of the forty-nine communities studied. In the survey, we included a question asking the local leaders if *any* important political debate had taken place in their locality within the previous three years. If they responded affirmatively, they were asked to specify the theme or themes of the debate. This question was intended initially to measure the ability of the communities studied to generate substantial debate at the local level, but it has also permitted examination of the variations in the themes of debate articulated within the forty-nine communities.[5] As the data in table 3.1 show, those leaders with multiple ties to intellectuals are the most likely to mention several different topics of political debate: *national* economic and social policy, *local* economic problems and initiatives, and *local* social problems are all mentioned substantially more often by the leaders with multiple ties to intellectuals than by leaders with no ties or simple ties. National political debates and campaigns are also mentioned slightly more often by the leaders enjoying multiple ties. Local politics itself is almost equally prevalent in the responses of leaders with multiple and simple ties; leaders with no ties to intellectuals are roughly half as likely as their more connected counterparts to mention local politics as a theme of important political debate.

The conclusion should be clear: where social ties establish multiple connections between local working-class leaders and intellectuals, debates over politics are more likely to emphasize a variety of themes, including both broadly experienced national policies and specific local problems. Leaders strongly connected to the world of intellectuals are inclined to raise issues and discuss problems that are both local and extralocal in scope. Political energies and dissatisfaction are, as a result, focused on the connections between directly experienced local problems and broad extralocal developments such as national economic policy, European integration, and so on. In sharp contrast, the leaders with no ties to intellectuals are actually the most likely to mention debates limited to general ideological or programmatic themes, without a specific tangible connection to their locality. Such tie-less leaders may mention abstract *or* localistic themes, but they are not typically predisposed to link the two in a rhetoric addressing but transcending locally felt problems. These survey responses standing alone cannot tell the whole story; the local histories and experiences conveyed in the course of numerous qualitative interviews, when coupled with the survey analysis, make it possible to see how some communities and leaders succeed in establishing linkages between the local and the extralocal. Still, the survey responses suggest that social ties substantially increase the propensity of the local leaders to link the specific to the general; the qualitative interviews make it possible for us to see how that propensity is manifested in the actual political life of the communities—how the issues and demands brought to public attention by the local leaders succeed or fail to engage widespread extralocal concerns while defending specific local interests.

Before beginning a more thorough exploration of the underlying causal mechanisms linking ties and discourse, let us first take up briefly one reasonably obvious avenue of analysis that might suggest substantial qualifications in the argument I propose. I leave largely for chapter 5 a systematic consideration of alternative explanations— or competing hypotheses—for the relationship here emphasized. But before we proceed, it will be useful to consider briefly this avenue of analysis.

Intellectuals and Ideological Thinking

Many readers might ask, on seeing the data linking social ties to discursive horizons, whether this pattern actually reflects the ability of intellectuals to persuade those with whom they interact to adopt a given ideological perspective or perspectives. Indeed, the capacity of intellectuals to shape, or reshape, the thinking of workers and others has been argued by many significant and diverse thinkers: Lenin, Tocqueville, Raymond Aron, Joseph Schumpeter, and Gramsci are only some of those who assert, in one fashion or another, that intellectuals generate substantial changes in the way that discontented individuals—workers or others—understand, formulate, and defend their interests.[6] Is, then, the tendency of some local leaders to link the local to the extralocal simply one specific manifestation of a more generalized embrace of an ideological perspective transmitted by intellectuals? The survey offers a clear opportunity to explore this question. The respondents were asked what the word *socialism* meant for them. Although the local working-class leaders interviewed represented a wide variety of perspectives, initiatives, and objectives, whether they were radicals or moderates they almost invariably defended their views from the standpoint of a socialist identity of one sort or another. Within the two ideological families of the contemporary Spanish Left—the socialist and the postcommunist subcultures—socialism is understood in a variety of different ways, but the mission of the Left is invariably seen as the pursuit of objectives somehow linked to that historic concept, whatever it might mean. In Bernardo Bertolucci's epic film treatment of the Italian workers' movement, *1900*, a desolate labor militant, forced to wander about while evading repression during the Fascist period, poignantly asks himself aloud, "Where is socialism?" Several decades later, the troubled query of many left militants had doubtless become "What is socialism?" In the absence of any clear consensus on the contemporary meaning of socialism, the interviewed leaders' interpretation of the term stands as a good yardstick of their ideological placement. Respondents were offered four choices: (1) a type of society fundamentally different from the current one in Western societies, (2) a set of values that can orient political action, (3) a probably never-ending process of the democratization of society and the reduction of injustices, and (4) the historical identity of a movement that has changed a great deal in recent decades.

TABLE 3.2
Meaning attributed to socialism by leaders, by ties to intellectuals

Socialism understood as:	No Ties (%)	Simple Ties (%)	Multiple Ties (%)	Total (%)
1. A fundamentally different society; unlike those in the contemporary West	13.2	11.4	10.8	11.7
2. Set of values that can orient political action	5.5	7.1	12.9	9.3
3. Never-ending process of democratization and of reducing inequalities	68.1	68.6	64.0	66.3
4. Historical identity of a movement that has changed greatly	11.0	12.9	10.8	11.3
5. Other answer; no answer	2.2	—	1.4	1.3
N	91	70	139	300

Note: To test for statistical significance, I created a dummy variable for each answer and tested it against social ties separately. The only statistically significant relationship found is between response 2 ("set of values that orient action") and social ties when using the linear-by-linear test of association, which reveals significance at $p = .05$. None of the other relationships reaches even the most marginal level of statistical significance.

The first of the four definitions of socialism clearly differs substantially from the other three. Only this first answer is consistent with the radical, or ideologically firm, commitment to "transcend" capitalism and/or to fundamentally transform contemporary society. The very limited support for the maximalist sense of socialism, as shown in table 3.2, will perhaps surprise those observers who would have assumed a broader commitment to fundamental social change on the part of local working-class leaders in a country such as Spain with a significant revolutionary past.[7] However, for our concerns the important finding here is not the absolute level of support for the radical or maximalist response but rather its distribution. Remarkably, the contacts between intellectuals and local working-class leaders make essentially no impact on the likelihood that the local leaders will embrace the maximalist sense of socialism. Support for the maximalist understanding of socialism varies by only 2.4%, from a low of 10.8% among respondents with multiple ties to intellectuals to a virtually identical figure, 13.2%, among respondents without ties to intellectuals. This tiny variation is clearly insufficient to sustain any argument attributing the ideological orientation of the local leaders to the intellectuals' influence. If the social ties between intellectuals and workers do indeed shape political life, the mechanism at work must take a substantially different form; contact with intellectuals does not generate a specific ideological vision on the part of the leaders. And presumably, the intellectuals have not persuaded the leaders to adopt a specific point of view. Somehow the social contacts we examine manage to reshape public rhetoric, but political or ideological "conversion" is not the mechanism underpinning this effect.

Subcultures: The Spheres of Worker–Intellectual Interaction

The two main subcultures of the Spanish Left, introduced in chapters 1 and 2, serve as partially enclosed contexts of interaction between intellectuals and workers. An intellectual whose identity and social ties place him or her in either of the two subcultures—even if he or she is not a formal member of the predominant party within the subculture—is likely to maintain working-class contacts exclusively or almost exclusively within that same subculture. If worker–intellectual ties reshape discursive horizons, as the data show, they must do so within subcultures, or at a minimum within one of the two subcultures. Thus it is essential to compare the impact of ties on discursive horizons within the two subcultures.

When we do examine the two subcultures separately, it becomes clear that substantial effects of worker–intellectual interactions emerge under some circumstances but not others. The (subculturally specific) understandings, expectations, and practices surrounding formally similar ties help to determine the magnitude—if any at all—of their causal effect. As the data in figure 3.2 show, the impact of the ties is far greater in the postcommunist subculture than in the sample taken as a whole; in the socialist subculture, no clear causal pattern emerges.

Within the postcommunist subculture, the propensity of local leaders to articulate globalizing discursive horizons is strongly related to their ties with intellectuals. Among unconnected leaders within the subculture, only 20.4% opt for globalizing discursive horizons. The preference for globalizing discourse rises powerfully with social ties, reaching its high point among the most connected leaders. Among leaders with limited contacts, the preference for globalizing discursive horizons rises to 44.8%; among those with multiple con-

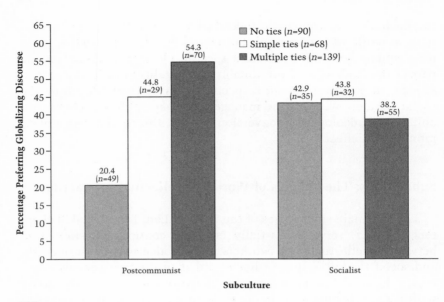

FIG. 3.2
Globalizing discursive horizons by leaders' ties to intellectuals for both subcultures.
When the relationship between the preference for a globalizing discourse and ties to
intellectuals is tested separately in each subculture, a highly significant relationship
(p = .001) is revealed only in the postcommunist subculture.

tacts with intellectuals, the figure is a substantially higher 54.3%.
Thus the predisposition to articulate global discursive horizons is
more than two and a half times as high among strongly connected
leaders as among the totally unconnected.

In the socialist subculture, the causal pattern is remarkably different. Indeed there is no effect at all to be discerned. Leaders with
simple ties to intellectuals are, by a small margin, those most likely
to embrace a globalizing discourse. Leaders with multiple ties are the
least likely to embrace such rhetorics, the reverse of our finding in
the postcommunist subculture. The phenomena at work within the
socialist subculture are doubtless complex, but for some reason or set
of reasons, ties between intellectuals and workers in this context lack
the causal impact discernable within the other subculture. The discussion of worker–intellectual ties in chapter 2 may shed some light
on this strong disparity in the pattern of causality: postcommunist
subculture leaders were more inclined than their socialist subculture

counterparts to view the ties as useful. Moreover, the meaning placed in the ties, and in the efforts required to build them, appeared greater in the postcommunist subculture. At the time of my research, the ties of socialist subculture intellectuals and leaders with policy-makers in Madrid, where the Socialist Party held governmental power, were doubtless more highly valued than were linkages between intellectuals and local working-class leaders. Thus the ties carry their greatest causal significance where they—and the effort required to build them—are most highly valued. We explore this disparity between the two subcultures in greater depth in chapter 6.

Local Political Endeavors

Through the survey data we are able, in this and following chapters, to analyze the quantitative relations among variables, permitting us to draw conclusions about the causal patterns predisposing actors to given behaviors—such as articulating global discursive horizons. But how are those predispositions actually manifested in local political life? What forms does political life take in those localities inclined to articulate global discursive horizons? It is only through the actual experiences of the forty-nine communities, or at least some of them, that we can establish the full meaning in political life of the predispositions highlighted by the survey findings.

All of our forty-nine towns have their important local stories and experiences, but some of the communities offer especially telling instances of the general tendencies I have identified.[8] The mining and industrial towns set along the banks of the Nalón River in the northern region of Asturias offer countless specific examples of the very phenomena suggested in rough form by the survey data.[9] The urban form of Asturias, characterized in many instances by the consolidation in one municipality of several distinct yet nearby settlements, is quite unlike that of most of Spain. The Nalón's population of approximately 100,000 inhabitants in 1990 was heavily concentrated in towns belonging to the valley's two principal municipalities: Langreo, the largest, and San Martín del Rey Aurelio, with roughly half the population of its larger neighbor downriver. Much of the valley's life is organized in its various settlements: Sotrondio, El Entrego, and others belonging to the municipality of San Martín; La Felguera, Sama, and others belonging to the Nalón's largest munici-

pality, Langreo. Because our primary concern lies with the nature of
political life organized at the municipal level rather than the social
life set in the bars and plazas of the various settlements, we will focus
here on the valley's life through its two principal municipalities
rather than on the larger number of individual settlements. Both of
these two municipalities fall within the overall pool of forty-nine
industrial towns included in the survey; Mieres, the primary municipality of the neighboring mining valley the Caudal, also falls within
the study, although it stands in marked contrast to the municipalities of the Nalón.

The survey responses establish both of the Nalón's primary municipalities, Langreo and San Martín, as unusually high in the level of
contact between local working-class leaders and intellectuals. Many
of those whom I interviewed happily related the local legend that a
UNESCO study carried out in the 1960s had identified the valley as
the home of "the square kilometer with the highest cultural level in
all Europe."[10] In many respects the Nalón strikes the sociological
observer as a coherent unit with an identifiable pattern characterizing its collective life, but the political reality, for those active in the
valley's public life, is far more complex. Numerous political differences separate those active in the towns nestled between the steep
hills and mountains surrounding the valley. Within the postcommunist subculture, the leading figures in San Martín and Langreo rarely
find themselves on the same side of the political and factional dis-
putes found within their subculture's union and principal party. At
the time of the survey, San Martín's local leadership tended to
support and Langreo's local leadership tended to oppose the then-
dominant line within the regional Asturian organizations of the
postcommunist subculture. Thus, the shared sociological pattern I
identify within the valley cannot be attributed to the predominance
of any one given political tendency or factional grouping. An
informed observer, familiar with the political history of the valley,
might be tempted to attribute my principal findings—the linkage to
intellectuals and the global discursive horizons articulated in the
Nalón's politics—to the role of specific individuals important in
the valley and particularly in Langreo. Indeed, we must take note of
the individual contribution of Langreo's former mayor, Aladino
Fernández, now a professor of geography in the provincial capital,
Oviedo, who was elected in 1983 as a Socialist. Many valley leaders

active in both subcultures still mention their fondness for Fernández and their respect for both his academic achievements and his continuing concern for the valley. We could also note the distinctive political abilities—and discursive horizons—of Alberto Rubio, area-wide secretary general of CCOO for the valley at the time of the interviews, before his successful candidacy for the regional leadership of CCOO in 1996. These individuals—and others whose political involvements began in Langreo—are indeed important to the valley's history. But the discursive spirit and the social linkages found throughout the valley are in no sense a simple reflection of two or three leaders from Langreo, as the politics of its smaller neighbor, San Martín, clearly shows.

On February 9 and 10, 1990, the local branch of Izquierda Unida in San Martín, just upriver from Langreo, held a small conference titled "Mining and Its Surroundings."[11] The invited speakers, in the sessions held in this mining municipality of some 25,000 inhabitants at the time, included a historian, a professor of literature, two doctors, a business association representative, and several local political leaders of Izquierda Unida. From the theme of miners in literature to the specific problems faced by women in the minefields and the question of mining and the environment, the issues discussed were extraordinarily wide ranging. The objective of reindustrialization was a central concern in the conference, but it did not crowd out other themes of political importance. This thoughtfully organized conference was no exception; it expresses in clear form major features of politics in San Martín and in the valley as a whole. Leaders and activists in San Martín have displayed considerable independence from the larger municipality of Langreo, frequently launching their own political initiatives, often placing themselves in opposition to the line or strategy dominant just downriver. Although second in population and political importance within the valley, San Martín has been fully capable of sustaining ties to intellectuals, fully able to articulate its political agenda through global discursive horizons.

The spirit of the February conference was sustained in various other activities in San Martín during 1990. On June 13 of that same year, a young historian native to the town, Ramón García Piñeiro, read a manifesto in the public square in front of city hall on behalf of a local reindustrialization coalition organized by the town's branch of Izquierda Unida.[12] In the manifesto, the coalition called for the use of public funds to create new and lasting employment in industries with a future. The manifesto insisted that no mines should be closed until public policies were in place guaranteeing an alternative economic future. After criticizing as ineffective certain existing industrial uses of state funds, the statement read by García Piñeiro proclaimed, "We must insist that public resources are used to generate lasting employment, secure employment, permanent employment."[13] Local human problems, as well as state and regional policies, were all touched on in the manifesto's call for reindustrialization. While the manifesto was being read in the town square, Izquierda Unida town council members were presenting the municipality's representative body with a twelve-page document analyzing local, national, and international dimensions of the area's industrial decline and proposing policy initiatives intended to reverse the process. In a public roundtable discussion organized by the local reindustrialization coalition in November of the same year, a number of fairly practical themes were raised: the future infrastructural requirements of the entire region of Asturias, the need for local entrepreneurs, national governmental policy and the future of specific firms, and comparisons with efforts at reindustrialization outside the borders of Spain. The economist, historian, and engineer participating in the roundtable connected the locality's pressing employment crisis to translocal themes. The crucial rhetorical question was posed quite directly by Angel Manuel Arias, a mining engineer: "Can San Martín, on its own, build alternatives to industrial decline?"[14] The Nalón's response to that question is no mystery: the political initiatives emerging from both Langreo and San Martín clearly reflect the operating assumption of the valley's predominant working-class leaders—that acting alone and focusing only on specific local problems, they could not forge successful alternatives to industrial decline. But in those local contexts without ties to intellectuals, the implicit response to the mining engineer's rhetorical question would be sharply different; only a few kilometers away in the Caudal valley (conventionally placed alongside the Nalón in sociological and political analyses of Asturias, as if the two valleys were largely indistinguishable from one another), various struggles aimed at keeping specific mines open stand as a clear reminder that defensive localism can orient popular energies and discontent just as easily as the global discursive horizons of the Nalón.

Under the leadership of miner Javier Arjona, San Martín's local branch of Izquierda Unida consistently attempted to address both broad extralocal problems and specificities of the municipality. In *Concejo*, IU's engaging but somewhat irregularly (and infrequently) produced local publication, this dual concern for the local and the extralocal was constantly evident. A roughly printed edition of *Concejo* from 1993, in addition to its concern for San Martín, focused on two broad national or even international objectives pursued and discussed at the global level: the call for a shortened workweek and the goal of sustainable development. A simple statement, reflecting on the challenge faced by the municipality and its surroundings, highlights the political spirit predominant within the valley:

> Some regions experiencing industrial restructuring have organized very hard struggles in defense of jobs, defensive union struggles, that have ended often in defeat. The question, then, would not be to defend jobs as such, in a world in which changes take place so quickly, but rather [to defend] the right to Live and Work in one's own country, in one's region. That is to say to create New Jobs, to Reindustrialize, vocational training courses, Offensive and not defensive solutions.[15]

By January 1994, the San Martín Branch was able to produce a more glossy issue of *Concejo*, twelve pages in length. The contents of the publication, divided into a number of stories and items on many different themes, offer us no real surprise, given the prior endeavors of the town's IU branch: specific items on particular local problems, including schools and housing, could be found alongside discussions of Third World development and other concerns transcending the valley's borders. Both local problems and worldwide trends were featured in the political initiatives and the public discourse launched by local leaders in this community of miners.

The political activities initiated within the relatively small municipality of San Martín are indeed noteworthy, but the most widely visible campaigns, the most politically salient endeavors, emerged from the Nalón's largest municipality, Langreo. The two large union confederations, UGT and CCOO, both maintain valleywide union headquarters in Langreo. In a valley with a history of major—frequently violent—labor conflicts throughout the twentieth century, the party and municipal council leaders of Langreo must share the political spotlight with the Nalón's union leadership headquartered in the locality. The Nalón valley's branch of Comisiones Obreras has assumed a position of special importance, launching major campaigns and initiatives intended to defend the interests and the future of the valley's residents. Under the leadership of Alberto Rubio, valleywide secretary general of CCOO until his election to secretary general for Asturias as a whole on an insurgent slate in 1996, Comisiones Obreras has placed the problems of unemployment and deindustrialization in a broadly comparative light. Reindustrialization has been the central demand of CCOO, and through the pursuit of this objective the local union federation has challenged government policy and economic forces at work both within and beyond the valley's borders. CCOO has typically attempted to place the valley's plight in the broadest possible terms; union publications, such as the local organization's carefully drafted summary report published in 1994, typically refer to the mining valleys in the plural—rather than focusing specifically on mine closures in the Nalón.

Rubio was quite conscious of the globalizing spirit informing the Nalón's collective endeavors: "We tie our problematic, what is happening here, to the general problematic, away from here. . . . It is important to globalize, but on the basis of the specificity of places."[16] The discourse of this able union leader was constantly infused with both tangible local references and translocal themes. "I know that we are not an island. We have the same problems as Mieres [in the neighboring Caudal valley, where defensive localism predominated]. . . . We have to resolve our problems through what unites us with others, through the problems that unite us with others. . . . I do not talk of the Ventura mine or the Entrego mine. We talk about HUNOSA [the state-owned company that held virtually all the major mines in Asturias]."[17] In addressing the problems faced by the miners of HUNOSA, and by other industrial workers as well as the unemployed, Rubio ended up posing various extralocal themes. When articulating to the press the rationale for a locally initiated general strike held on March 23, 1993 (also supported by the Caudal), the union leader explicitly tied this labor protest to both national government policy and broader historical lessons. The general strike, he insisted, would "place in question the economic policy of the Government." He warned, moreover, that "the contained anger of citizens could explode" and that unemployed workers had contributed to the rise of Nazism in Germany.[18]

One would hardly anticipate finding a differing story in the adjacent—and by conventional criteria, quite similar—mining valley, but my research findings underscore the existence of just such a difference. The Caudal's contrasting embrace of defensive localism is evident not only in the vigorous mobilizational efforts to keep open specific mines such as Santa Bárbara, Barredo, and others, but also in the discursive horizons and strategic orientations of local leaders I interviewed in the valley. Javier, a CCOO leader in Mieres, notes that a couple of years before the PSOE's 1982 victory, when confronted with the threat of an economically induced closure at the Fábrica de Mieres, the town responded with a locally focused campaign opposing the shutdown. The focus of this effort, as summarized by its slogan, could not be clearer: "Let us all save Mieres!" This very concrete emphasis on maintaining a *specific* local source of employment was not to be an isolated event. The same leader notes that following the Socialist victory in 1982, virtually every year saw a major union struggle in which "principally everything was organized around the defense of [local] jobs." The defense of jobs in the Caudal, as Javier explained, was pursued through mobilizations intending to prevent specific mine closures, and he added, "it is important to continue struggling for this." On occasion, Caudal activists did attempt to articulate or endorse globalizing discursive horizons, but such efforts were not sustained, and they clearly absorbed much less of this valley's mobilizational efforts than its more prominent defensive localist campaigns. Javier remembered that a reindustrialization initiative had been attempted in the Caudal, but, he noted, it failed to obtain the resonance of similar campaigns in the Nalón. As the Mieres unionist explained: "Here it did not lead to results." Thus he quite explicitly defended the Caudal's preference for mobilizational efforts, "prioritizing the local, the singular."[19] Javier, like other leaders in similarly localist settings, argued that townspeople were more easily drawn into such singular, or particularist, struggles, and indeed the Caudal's history shows that many such protests had elicited mass participation. To underscore the point, he noted with evident pride the massive and well-publicized (yet unsuccessful) local campaign to keep open the Barredo pit.

The fundamental contrast between the Nalón's globalizing spirit and the Caudal's localistic perspective manifests itself in numerous ways, large and small. Alongside the crisis of industrial decline and severe job loss, the environmental challenges faced by the two valleys offer us a useful opportunity to witness differences between these adjacent contexts. In 1994, local officials in the Nalón's largest municipality, Langreo, arranged an exchange of ecological worker-trainees with Italy, thus making use of a European Union program promoting the training of workers in environmental control techniques.[20] Earlier that same year, ecologists in the Caudal's principal municipality, Mieres, had focused their efforts on suing the city government of Mieres itself in connection with the municipal waste dump. The local Freixó environmentalist group, as an Asturian newspaper reported, asked a judge to force the Mieres city council "to repair the damages caused to the inhabitants of the area and to order a clean-up of the affected place at the expense of municipal funds."[21] Similar reflections of this underlying contrast can be found in other issue domains as well. Just two days earlier, the Mieres branch of the Asturian nationalist Partiu Asturianista had criticized the city government for facilitating the construction of a large local shopping center, which, the nationalists alleged, would end up endangering the survival of existing local commercial establishments.[22] At the same time, local actors in the Nalón frequently had their sights focused on horizons far beyond their valley's boundaries. In the summer of 1994, Saharan and Senegalese children traveled to Langreo to spend the summer as guests of valley residents.[23] In a similar spirit, the city governments of both Langreo and smaller San Martín raised funds from both the municipal coffers and individual local residents to be sent to Rwanda in support of relief efforts there. The mayor of San Martín issued a "call to [local] inhabitants, reminding them of the bad situation being experienced in that country and asking for their solidarity with poverty in the world so they would contribute to the extent of their possibilities."[24] Many small episodes and initiatives reflect the underlying contrast between the two valleys' discursive horizons.

Nonetheless, it would be both unfair and inaccurate to portray the Caudal as a cultural and discursive wasteland. Even in the Caudal, some intellectuals and workers had attempted to forge connections; some local actors on occasion articulated globalizing visions, but such endeavors did not prove sustainable and thus failed to take hold (as Javier's comments, reported earlier, suggested). In 1994 Caudal residents offered touching tributes to the efforts of one longtime valley resident—author, literary scholar, and high school principal Carmen Díaz Castañón—who had organized various lectures and cultural activities in Mieres prior to her death in early July. Among the friends who eulogized her were prominent intellectual and literary figures from outside the valley, such as philosopher Gustavo Bueno, who strongly criticized a 1991 government investigation of the high school she directed, which, he claimed, ended in her resignation.[25] The late educator's project for the valley had been educational, cultural, as well as discursive. She is said to have once remarked, "For Mieres, I ask for *conversation*, a conversation that moves beyond ferocious particular ambitions, the crude interests of a few, in order to focus on more generic matters."[26]

Exactly why the efforts of Carmen Díaz Castañón and others within the Caudal failed to engender strong intellectual–worker ties and globalizing discursive horizons in that setting is a question more for monographic local history than a broader study such as this one. Perhaps her decision to remain a political independent, despite the efforts of some on the Left to attract her to their ranks, helps to explain that outcome. The political life and discourse of the Caudal have been strongly channeled by the organizations and activists of the two left subcultures here emphasized. Yet for whatever reason, the pattern of intellectual–worker ties (or more precisely, their virtual absence) and the dominant conversation in the Caudal were quite unlike those to be found in the neighboring Nalón.

Before closing our discussion of the mining valleys, it is worth emphasizing that some Caudal activists did explicitly lament their valley's reigning localism and attempted in one way or another (but without meaningful success) to initiate broader and translocal endeavors.[27] If this book's central argument is correct, viable ongoing social connections contribute at least as much as the underlying preferences of isolated leaders and activists to building a terrain in which globalizing discursive horizons can flourish.

Discursive Horizons Where Labor Is Moderate

The sharp contrast between the (equally militant) adjacent mining valleys of Asturias finds some parallels in the differences between two nearby textile towns in the far more moderate Valencian region: historic Alcoi in the province of Alicante and, just over the Sierra of Mariola, the somewhat smaller textile town of Ontinyent in Valencia province.[28] The survey responses of local leaders in the two towns establish Alcoi as a community with unusually frequent ties between intellectuals and workers, whereas Ontinyent is a community relatively lower in those linkages. Qualitative interviewing in the two towns confirmed that survey finding; as a municipal councilor of Izquierda Unida (Esquerra Unida del País Valencià, or EU, in the Valencian region) explained, "At the local level, the relationship between intellectuals and our organization is fairly uncommon. That relationship doesn't exist here in Ontinyent."[29] In sharp contrast to the view expressed in Ontinyent, municipal leaders of Izquierda Unida in Alcoi pointed to "the theoretical reflection that has been carried out in the organization in contact with prestigious people—historians, economists, etc." Who were these intellectuals, or "prestigious people," in the words of local leaders? The experience of the IU leaders was clear on this point: "They tend to be people originally from Alcoi who are now working away from here."[30]

Among the objectives stressed by local IU leaders was the development of an economic strategy for Alcoi focused, at a minimum, on the district as a whole (*la comarca*) rather than on the municipality by itself, and the ecological protection of the Sierra of Mariola separating their town from Ontinyent. Tellingly, Alcoi's globalizers attempted to build collective efforts with their counterparts in Ontinyent to further the environmental defense of the Mariola range, but they found the interest of their more localistic neighbors insufficient to sustain joint action.[31] A long document prepared by Alcoi IU leaders in 1993, to contribute to the debate on the state of their city, posed a wide range of issues from the highly concrete question of local industrial land use to broader perspectives on economics and politics. The globalizing horizons of Alcoi emerged clearly: "Very poorly can the problems affecting a large number of municipalities be resolved on the basis of action from and for just one of them." Although in discussing economic development strategies the Alcoi globalizers emphasized the importance of the district, rather than the municipality itself, they also looked beyond their own district: "Action restricted to the context of the current district . . . may end up being insufficient. The logic of economic development obliges political actions in this field to have, now, a territorial scope sufficiently broad to guarantee their effectiveness and relatively limited to guarantee public and democratic control."[32] Alongside their discourse emphasizing pragmatic areawide economic development strategies, Alcoi's IU leadership also presented numerous motions in the city council chambers on a variety of themes: the proposal to establish a full-fledged university in the area; support for a conscientious objector to military service (*insumiso*) from neighboring (localistic) Ontinyent; and a broad critique of national economic policy calling for increased governmental negotiation with unions and a more complete convergence with other European countries.[33]

The secretary general of CCOO for Alcoi also stressed the importance of links between his organization and intellectuals, mentioning as an example recent discussions with a university professor from Alicante concerning the potential contribution of new technologies to the economic future of this old textile town.[34] Among the concerns of CCOO's local organization in Alcoi was how to compete successfully with textile production in low-wage countries of the developing world. The union discussed several possibilities for confronting this challenge, including innovations in production techniques and districtwide strategies of economic development. The local secretary general was quite explicit about his globalizing perspective on the problems faced by industry in Alcoi and its surroundings: "There are not going to be magic solutions for each country individually . . . [solutions] have to be drawn out in a more globalized way."[35] The Alcoi labor movement was especially proud to have hosted an international meeting in the summer of 1994, bringing together textile-sector unionists from several countries ringing the Mediterranean. The international meeting, intended to help the sector's unions coordinate strategies, seemed an impressive undertaking for this middle-sized aging textile town ringed by mountains. Although the institutional sponsorship responsible for the meeting rested with the nationwide textile federations of CCOO and UGT, the local hosts in Alcoi collaborated in the event's organization and were proud to have been chosen as the site of this international encounter. Alcoi, just like the Nalón, placed its own problems in a broad framework transcending the local context.

In neighboring Ontinyent, much as in the Caudal, leaders typically spoke a more localistic discourse. The secretary general of CCOO for the town put it this way: "Here in Ontinyent we mobilize more around the concrete problem."[36] The secretary general of IU for the town mentioned as significant two demands of the postcommunist group: the construction of a highway bypass and the creation of more green park areas within the municipality.[37] Reasonable as those two objectives may seem, they clearly lack the globalizing spirit of IU leaders in Alcoi, just over the Mariola mountain range. Localism was also to be found in other towns of the Valencian region, as some of those we interviewed lamented. A relatively globalizing leader of IU in Elda complained that during regional meetings of his postcommunist political formation, "There are people who say that [given] the problems they have in their own town, why do they have to concern themselves with others?"[38] Thus both localistic and globalizing discursive horizons are to be found in the Valencian region.

One need not rely on the experiences of relatively isolated industrial communities such as the textile towns of the Valencian region or the mining valleys of Asturias to find compelling manifestations in actual political life of the linkage between social ties and discursive horizons. A useful complement to the stories related by leaders in Valencia and Asturias can be found in the metropolitan area of Barcelona, the greatest industrial concentration in Spain. Specific instances of defensive localism can be readily encountered in workplaces and localities scattered throughout the metropolitan area: banners demanding the protection of *particular* factories and jobs from the threat of closure or dismissal attest to the continuing appeal within Barcelona's working class of defensive localism and the limited discursive horizons it entails. In the numerous industrial communities of Barcelona's metropolitan area, our survey encountered evidence of a wide range of variation in the intensity of ties between intellectuals and workers—from virtually nonexistent ties in some localities to a high level of contact in others.

In contrast to the banners proclaiming defensive localist demands in all their narrow specificity, at other points in the Barcelona metropolitan area the political energies of communities and leaders that were tied to intellectuals offer numerous—and highly varied—examples of global discursive horizons. Perhaps most telling, for our purposes, is the distinctive political style of the "ex-Bandera" group of union and political leaders in the large and industrially diverse Baix Llobregat district. Unlike the union and political activists of the Asturian mining valleys, this group of leaders has been characterized by increasing moderation during the post-Franco period; yet similar to the militant leaders of the Nalón and the generally pragmatic leaders of Alcoi, the Bandera group has been consistently committed to broadly focused and yet locally grounded politics articulated through global discursive horizons. On issues ranging from unemployment to democratization and numerous other themes large and small, the leaders of the Baix Llobregat consistently attempted to address concrete local concerns through the lens of extralocal proposals and analyses. Their globalizing rhetorics rested on the foundation of unusually tight intellectual–worker linkages initially forged in the opposition movement during the late Franco period. For many Catalan intellectuals and political activists, the Baix Llobregat came to hold a certain mystique—with its origins in the struggles and victories of the anti-Franco movement within the district under the difficult constraints of authoritarian repression.[39] Journalist and author Manuel Campo Vidal, who lived there for a period of twenty years, underscored this point in a 1996 lecture delivered within the district: "During that period, the attraction of the Baix Llobregat was so powerful that there was a political migration, not to other countries but from Barcelona to the Baix Llobregat. . . . The attraction of the Baix was such that some of us, who in that period were students at the University of Barcelona, scarcely participated in student struggles because we had our commitment here [in the district]."[40]

Despite their relatively small numbers, the Bandera group held the dominant position within CCOO's Baix Llobregat district organization for roughly twenty years, from the late Franco period until the early 1990s.[41] The origins of this clearly defined group lay in Bandera Roja, a small Maoist party of the anti-Franco movement, which enjoyed its greatest strength in the Barcelona metropolitan area, especially in two seemingly dissimilar bases of support: one among students in the city's principal university and the other among workers in heavily industrial Cornellà, the largest municipality of the Baix Llobregat. During the late authoritarian years, the ranks of Bandera's members included a number of individuals who would later gain prominence in public life, once democracy returned: Jordi Sole Tura, a drafter of the new democratic constitution while a communist, and later minister of culture in a socialist government; Jordi Borja, urban theorist and municipal politician; Alfonso Carlos Comín, the prominent left-Catholic theorist and writer; Juan García Nieto, the worker-priest, sociologist, and educator as well as founder of Cornellà's Fundació Utopía; Carlos Navales, the union leader turned politician; and various university professors well known for scholarly achievements within their fields. For most veterans of Bandera's anti-Franco efforts, the human community and social ties forged in opposition to dictatorship were to prove more enduring than the Maoist ideology officially characterizing their organization.

During the transition from authoritarianism to democracy, the majority of Bandera Roja decided to join the substantially larger Communist Party, that is, the PCE in most of Spain, or the allied PSUC in Catalonia. Within the Communist Party, the ex-Bandera members soon became known for their strong defense of the Eurocommunist redefinition of the communist legacy.[42] Their more hard-line opponents within Spanish communism insisted that their rapid political evolution had quickly placed them in the social democratic tradition; some among their opponents even redubbed their tendency *bandera blanca* or "white flag" instead of the initial *bandera roja* or "red flag." There is no need to relate here in greater detail—much less, to evaluate—this evolution toward the most moderate positions found within the postcommunist tradition. What should be underscored for our purposes is that the ex-Bandera group constituted a relatively cohesive set of working-class leaders, highly connected to the world of intellectuals and clearly placed in the most moderate positions possible within the postcommunist political tradition; indeed, on an individual basis many ex-Bandera leaders would ultimately switch their party allegiance to the Socialists, often maintaining their union allegiance to CCOO, and thus serving as a (relatively exceptional) "bridge" between the two subcultures otherwise structurally separate from one another.

The global discursive horizons of the ex-Bandera group have been manifested in speeches, assemblies, and meetings addressing economic and social policy as well as the fundamental political goal of building democracy in post-Franco Spain. Much like their more radical counterparts of the Nalón, the globalizers of the Baix have consistently sought to establish connections between locally felt problems and broadly focused (extralocal) programs or initiatives. For the moderate Bandera group, during the founding years of Spain's post-Franco democracy, the determined defense of peak-level sociopolitical pacts—such as the Moncloa Pacts of 1977 and the Acuerdo Nacional sobre el Empleo (ANE) of 1981—constituted a clear example of their approach to politics. Speaking to assembled workers at a pre–May Day union rally in Cornellà on April 30, 1982, Emilio García, at the time the districtwide secretary general of CCOO, implored those present to see the recently enacted extended unemployment benefits and other tangible, if small, improvements for workers as the result of the unions' *nationwide* strategy of negotiation and restraint.[43] Concrete individual benefits and nationwide political strategies such as economywide concertation were inextricably linked in the discourse of Bandera leaders. This perspective contributed at the time to the political isolation of the Bandera group within the then substantially more radical Barcelona labor movement.[44] The Baix Llobregat highlights how moderate political objectives may be defended through the global discursive horizons of working-class leaders. As the contrasts and similarities between the Baix and the Nalón suggest, the reach of political rhetoric—but not its ideological cast—is shaped by the presence or absence of social ties such as those emphasized here.

It is worth emphasizing that the moderation of the Baix was manifested in support for concertation not only at the nationwide level but also within the district itself. The local branch of CCOO played a crucial role in the pioneering effort to set down a districtwide framework for negotiation, cooperation, and institutional innovation linking unions, employers, and local governments.[45] Union and political leaders were proud of their effort to build a concertation framework focusing on concrete local projects involving employment training and other economic development objectives. Thus globalizers in the Baix sought to pursue multilevel efforts encompassing mundane matters emerging in specific workplaces, districtwide negotiation and developmental strategies, nationwide political commitments and negotiations—as well as still-broader horizons.

CCOO leaders in the district articulated this complex globalizing vision with care in the general report they issued late in 1989, presenting in unmistakable terms their fundamental approach to labor politics: "We should also be capable of advancing the idea that all workers need to situate our demands in a broader perspective, that the current level of development of multinationals and the process of European economic integration demand a broader framework of negotiation." In their analysis, the union leaders discussed a wide range of issues, including industrial development and concertation in the Baix itself, local water use issues, the district's connection to the broader problems of the Barcelona metropolitan area, and—as readers will have come to expect—both national and international agendas. Nonetheless, they never lost sight of tangible challenges in the individual workplaces in which their membership was to be found, and

thus they insisted on the need to rigorously enforce negotiated contract provisions: "We are not among those who are satisfied to sign
[contracts] allowing things to be enforced on their own. . . . we have
always insisted that labor's struggle does not end with the signing of
a good contract, that it is perhaps more difficult to maintain and
broaden our victories on a day by day basis." The Baix globalizers
again manifested the broad reach and range of their concerns in their
call for "the defense of environmental conditions, understood as
a struggle to improve the environment both within and outside
the factory, and which today has instruments available such as demanding the application of European Union legislation [normativas
comunitarias]."[46]

Perhaps even more interesting than the broad commitments—
including macrolevel moderation, mesolevel concertation, and
numerous others—of the district's leaders was their ingenuity in
using global discursive horizons to translate small locally felt incidents into support for large national causes. In January 1984, elected
union delegates in a firm located in the district town of Viladecans
faced dismissal by their employer, despite the formal legal prohibition against the firing of workers for union activity. The Baix Llobregat district organization of CCOO responded with a broad
campaign intended both to gather support for the specific union delegates dismissed and to pose the general issue of democratic legal
freedoms for union activity. CCOO distributed informational sheets
announcing the court hearing scheduled for February 2, 1984. The
labor organization called on workers to attend the legal proceedings
to demonstrate support for the dismissed delegates and to rally
behind workers' basic right to union activity. The argument presented in the widely circulated leaflet spoke at both levels: that of
the particular delegates dismissed and that of the broader principles
at stake. After introducing the specific case of the Viladecans dismissals, the leaflet continued:

> The result of this hearing is very important to solidify the basis for
> union freedoms in this country. The issue is whether the company can
> control the union activity of the workers' representatives and the use
> those representatives make of the rights and guarantees recognized by
> the law, or if this prerogative belongs to the workers and unions who
> have chosen them.[47]

The leaflet then briefly relates the specific incident of Viladecans before reemphasizing the general theme:

> In our opinion a union delegate's duty lies only and exclusively with the workers who have elected him. It is not by chance that the Workers' Statute leaves in the hands of the workers both the election process and the ability to revoke their representatives. It is a basic law for union freedom.

For the districtwide union leaders of the Baix Llobregat, the defense of worker representatives in one firm and the consolidation of democratic freedoms for unionism at the national level were strongly interconnected: to defend one cause was to defend the other. And the best way to advance this agenda was by linking the two issues—the local dismissal of worker representatives and the nation-wide goal of reaffirming newly reestablished freedoms for unionism—in their public appeal for support, as they did in this case. Thus even a specific problem in one local firm afforded an opportunity to raise broad political issues, in this case democratic rights for unions. The moderate Bandera group focused heavily on the sometimes mundane defense of highly specific worker interests, but in doing so it employed global discursive horizons that constantly raised broad issues intended to be meaningful for publics not directly touched by the specific interests being defended. The politics of democratic transition and consolidation, peak-level negotiation and labor restraint, district-level concertation and development strategies (connected to translocal processes and policies); the defense of pro-labor policies in national debates coupled with the detailed focus on daily realities within the district's workplaces; and mobilizations in defense of legal rights for unionism: this list offers but a sampling of the wide range of globalizing discursive horizons articulated by leaders and activists in the Baix Llobregat.

The radical leaders of the Nalón, the pragmatists of Alcoi, and the moderates of the Baix Llobregat all employed global discursive horizons, thus contributing to political debate and dialogue not only within but also beyond their communities. Defensive localist leaders in towns neighboring these three contexts instead spoke only of limited hyperlocal concerns. Yet those defensive localists frequently did disrupt life beyond their towns, as the case of Linares tellingly illustrates. Labor-oriented protest has been a prominent component of Spanish democracy, but it has taken both directions—that of defensive localism as in the Caudal or of globalizing discursive horizons as in the Nalón. In this chapter I have argued that this fundamental contrast is explained in part by the prevalence of boundary-crossing social ties such as the intellectual–worker connections we examine, but we shall now explore alternatives to this claim.

4 Social Capital or Social Ties?

This book's argument that locally based social relations shape democracy's public life might seem to fit the theoretical spirit of scholars—such as the influential Robert Putnam and numerous others—who emphasize the explanatory power of what they call "social capital."[1] Such scholars would be inclined to conceive of the social ties we emphasize as but one component, one manifestation, of a broader underlying range of phenomena that, according to their arguments, tend to facilitate democratic performance, economic development, educational achievement, and other important outcomes. In their line of theorization, such diverse phenomena as trust, associational life, civic involvement, and other types of social relations all represent "social capital" that enables both individual actors and collective entities such as towns or regions to achieve felicitous outcomes in various endeavors. For "social capital" theorists, intellectual–worker ties would likely be seen as but one instance of the allegedly more important and deeper phenomenon they emphasize. Their perspective thus suggests a broad and challenging critique that requires our careful consideration: perhaps we *could* better explain the quality of democratic public life as reflected in discursive horizons by exploring the causal impact of the wide array of phenomena held to constitute "social capital." Thus "social capital" theory offers a clear explanatory alternative that we shall shortly examine though empirical analysis, but it is not easy to resolve through empirical analysis alone the choice between a broad and comprehensive operationalization of "social capital" or our more specific focus on the causal impact of particular types of social relations, be they worker–intellectual ties or others. We shall devote considerable time to reviewing the conceptual issues as well as the empirical evidence relevant for the choice between "social capital" analysis and the approach advanced in this book.

Examining the Concept of Social Capital

Despite the extraordinary attention the social capital concept has gained throughout the social sciences in recent years, and the unquestionable scholarly excellence of much work on this theme, the concept is open to serious critical evaluation. I argue that although virtually all the phenomena studied under this conceptual heading deserve the attention they currently attract, the social capital concept itself is not a useful way to frame such work and indeed creates unnecessary confusion. The simple case I make is that the explanatory work of social scientists is best served when we study the causal impact of *particular types of social relations* instead of placing all causally relevant social relations under one comprehensive conceptual heading, "social capital."

I ask readers to accept two small assertions as a reasonable basis for our examination of the social capital concept. First, as more than one professor has insisted in class, in principle it is a good idea for social scientists to "know what we are talking about."[2] Rigorous empirical analysis is essential for scientific progress, but it is of little or no use if we do not know what our empirical measures actually represent or capture. In the same vein, the conceptual ordering of the world is an important task of social science, but conceptual arguments ill serve us if we fail to establish the actual meaning of the concepts we deploy. Thus if the concept of social capital is to serve us well, we clearly must know what it means, hardly a controversial claim. Second, we absolutely must recognize that the simple coining of a term and framing of a concept do not, by themselves, demonstrate the existence of a meaningful underlying phenomenon—a point all too often forgotten by many social scientists. Concepts, as Max Weber elegantly insisted in his most influential methodological essay, are useful if they help us make sense out of underlying empirical reality, but concepts by themselves are not real things. They are only tools. Thus it is appropriate to ask whether the concept of social capital is a useful tool for studying empirical reality.

The proliferation of work organized around the social capital concept has not been accompanied by a matching consensus over the meaning of the term. Although many proponents of "social capital" analysis have elaborated the sense in which they use the term—in some instances with great theoretical force—collectively they have failed to develop a shared understanding of what it is they are talking about. Typically the term may be taken to refer to (a) social relations (which is to say, social ties, networks, and organizations) capable of generating useful resources for individual and collective actors; (b) socially rooted attitudes, norms, and understandings that promote cooperation; or (c) some combination of (a) and (b). Surely the most important theorization in American sociology is the seminal formulation of James Coleman, who understood "social capital" to refer to social relations or social structures that serve "as resources that can be used by actors to realize their interests." Nonetheless, Coleman's formulation is but one of various competing uses of the term, as is clear from recent excellent overviews of the relevant literature by Alejandro Portes, Michael Woolcock, and scholars outside the United States such as Arnaldo Bagnasco.[3]

Leaving aside, for a moment, the uncertainties posed by the tension between these multiple conceptual elaborations, it is important to underscore that most if not all the phenomena currently studied under the conceptual heading of "social capital" fully deserve the serious and sustained attention of social scientists that they currently enjoy. As a number of scholars writing on the concept have noted, "social capital" represents a (rather) new label to frame the study of phenomena that have long concerned sociologists and others.[4] Sociology as a discipline is built on the assumption that social relations help shape the human experience in ways that are subject to systematic study and understanding. The founding theorists of sociology and many contemporary empirical sociologists have made arguments that one can attempt to place under the broad conceptual umbrella offered by the "social capital" theorists—although it remains to be determined whether that great umbrella facilitates or impedes our search for understanding.

In a positive sense then, the "social capital" boom represents a growing interest of political scientists and economists in the explanatory contributions afforded by core themes in sociology. The attraction throughout the social sciences of this newly labeled package for studying a variety of important phenomena probably rests on its resonance with the language (and to a lesser extent, the assumptions) of economics and rational choice analysis. Nevertheless, this multidisciplinary diffusion of core sociological concerns comes at a considerable price. The importance of social relations is validated outside the field of sociology, but our collective ability to fully ascertain the causal impact of social relations is seriously impaired. This rather strained repackaging of largely sociological ideas in the language of economics creates several types of unnecessary confusion. I identify four problems of considerable magnitude in the growing use of this concept: (1) the unresolved confusion over its appropriate operationalization; (2) the misplaced assumption that "social capital" of different types can be understood to form an overall sum to which each component social relation (or norm) contributes in equivalent measurable units; (3) the loss of our ability to focus on contrasts in the causal logic generated by differing types of social ties or social relations; and (4) the probably irresolvable ambiguity over whether "social capital" should be understood to include only instrumentally constructed social relations or all causally relevant social relations. I do not take up here a rather different but intriguing objection that has recently been raised by left-oriented analysts, namely, the claim that capital should be understood to represent an inherently unequal economic relation and thus that it offers an inappropriate conceptual lens to study nonexploitative social relations.[5]

Let us take up first the issue of operationalization. The list of dimensions or aspects of social life that have been incorporated by one or another social scientist in overall measures of "social capital" is quite long, but there is no consensus over which items should be included or even over the principle to be followed in reaching that decision. In his two intellectually powerful books organized around the concept, Robert Putnam has employed substantially different operationalizations (although in the earlier work Putnam's "social capital"–like index is actually labeled a measure of the related concept of "civicness"). The complete list of components found in one or the other of those two indexes is both long and disparate.[6] Specific types of electoral participation, membership in formal organizations or in some subset of such organizations, actual participation in such organizations, informal social ties such as those connecting friends and family members, and attitudes of trust—all these and related items find a place in Putnam's trendsetting effort to operationalize the concept. In all, fourteen separate items are included in the comprehensive social capital index in *Bowling Alone*. The list is long, and it may well mask important distinctions for causal analysis such as—to take but one example—the contrast between the generalized trust of all others and the frequency of one's contact with friends. Other scholars employ different operationalizations, thus underscoring the confusion over what the concept's advocates actually take it to mean. Clearly if the concept is to prove genuinely useful, its defenders must be able to collectively specify how it should be operationalized and why we should choose some items for inclusion in a comprehensive measure. Whether that effort is possible or even desirable is an issue to which we shall now turn.

Can the Components of "Social Capital" Be Represented as a Meaningful Whole?

In most of the literature employing this concept, it is typically assumed that the various components of "social capital" constitute an overall sum or amount that can be meaningfully represented as a whole. Numerous works of scholarship purport to assess the overall amount, the total stock, or the general pool of "social capital" enjoyed by individuals or groups. Although some theoretical literature draws distinctions among what are seen as various types of "social capital," such distinctions have not lessened the general tendency of empirical work within this conceptual school to assume that an overall quantitative measure of total "social capital" can be meaningfully calculated and reported. Paradoxically, "social capital" scholars take note of potentially crucial contrasts between types of "social capital" and then proceed to develop comprehensive measures or yardsticks that effectively mask all distinctions among the various components of the overall phenomenon. Thus Putnam, in his most recent book, differentiates between what he calls "bonding" and "bridging" forms of "social capital"—arguing that they may act in substantially different ways—but that distinction does not deter him from formulating, and using extensively, a fourteen-item overall measure, his "comprehensive social capital index," to differentiate among American states in their total level of "social capital." Significant journal articles in more than one discipline do much the same, providing readers a multi-item generalized measure of total social capital as an integral part of their analyses of individual or community level phenomena. In this fashion, various components of an individual's or group's social relations (or understandings) are summed—or in some other way mathematically summarized—to form a comprehensive quantitative measure assumed to capture and represent the overall amount or stock of "social capital" available to the units under study, be they individuals, nations, or communities.

This assumption of the summability (or summarizability) of the diverse components of "social capital" into a meaningful whole, one that can be measured in units, is enormously convenient if valid but actually dangerous if not valid.[7] The assumption is a virtually inevitable by-product of the decision to use capital as a metaphor for conceptualizing and ordering the study of social relations (and understandings). Is this assumption valid? To answer that question, it will be useful to reflect on the differences between economic capital and what we are now encouraged to understand as "social capital."

Economic capital, as it is conventionally understood, encompasses various sorts of assets that firms or other economic actors may use to promote production and income. The capital of a firm, an individual, or a nation typically includes various components such as buildings, machinery, technological hardware, software, financial instruments or resources, and so on. The composition of a firm's capital (and thus the list of such components) will vary from case to case. Nonetheless, the list of components can be meaningfully added up *or* summarized in one overall measure. Granted, there may be competing approaches to summarizing a firm's overall capital resources: the book value and the market capitalization of a firm may diverge sharply. Nonetheless, both of these alternative measures offer us a meaningful summary assessment of a firm's worth. Our ability to specify the total amount of economic capital possessed by an actor rests on a simple and obvious foundation: differing types of capital assets are exchangeable for one another on the market. Capital assets have knowable (if sometimes unsteady) exchange value, and that value has a given monetary expression. The sphere of human relations to which economic capital pertains provides a unified metric for determining the value of all different types of capital assets. Moreover, that metric is meaningful for both economic actors and social scientists. Capital assets, in the economic realm, can be added up and meaningfully represented as an overall sum, a whole that is conventionally understood to be measurable in standard monetary units, and which is thus fungible.[8]

In contrast, the various facets of social life that we are now encouraged to understand as forming "social capital" cannot be exchanged for one another. One cannot trade in family ties in order to gain more acquaintances. One cannot exchange formal associational membership for informal social ties. One cannot exchange the predisposition to trust others (or to be trusted by them) for membership in a professional association. Thus there is some basis to question our ability to measure and add up the various alleged components of "social capital" through one meaningful metric.

Two qualifications to this observation deserve mention. First, individuals may indeed choose to exchange useful information and other resources gained through social relations. The reciprocal (but at times asymmetrical) exchange of favors and assistance represents an enduring feature of social life, more pronounced in some settings than others. Second, the construction and maintenance of social ties can easily involve an "opportunity cost" for the actors involved. The time spent in building professional ties may detract from family relations, and the reverse is also true.

Notwithstanding these two qualifications, it remains the case that social relations themselves—the alleged central components of "social capital," at least in the theoretical formulation by Coleman—cannot be exchanged in modern society. Genuinely close friendship and many other fundamental social relationships are not available for purchase or trade. Interestingly, each of the two qualifications introduced above could be seen to offer a potential basis for measuring "social capital" in meaningful units, but the two metrics are mutually contradictory. We could assign weights to social relations on the basis of the exchange value of resources (such as job availability information from an acquaintance, which others might obtain from an employment agency for a fee; advice from family or friends on how to prepare for a career, which the unconnected might have to pay to receive from expert consultants; and so forth) gained through those connections. Alternatively, we could assign weights in an overall index of social relations on the basis of the time spent in building—and sustaining—those social connections. Unfortunately this choice offers the index-builders no easy solution: the time or effort involved in building a social tie is often not correlated to the potential exchange value of resources (such as job search information) made available by the tie. We are left without a universally valid metric for establishing the contribution of various forms of social relations to one's presumed overall level of "social capital."

The Causal Impact of Social Relations: One Logic or Many Logics?

If it is indeed fruitful to conceive of causally relevant social relations as summable into one overall measure of "social capital," then we should be able to establish that our explanatory capacities are enhanced by focusing on that overall summary measure instead of on the specific underlying social relations we must measure and add up (or otherwise summarize in some quantitative fashion) to construct the overall index. However, just the reverse is the case. We lose considerable explanatory power by employing an overall measure of "social capital" instead of searching for the causal impact of specific types of social relations, each of them generating given consequences. "Social capital" would stand as a great conceptual innovation if we could demonstrate that, in its explanatory power, the whole is greater than the sum of its parts. I argue that in this case the whole is less than the sum of its parts because the whole—that is to say, a summary measure of "social capital"—masks the substantial (and differing) causal consequences of many specific types of social relations. As Stephen Smith and Jessica Kulynych insist in their recent critique, "the terminology of social capital oversimplifies the character of such relationships and actually obscures the vast differences in their effects."[9] The carefully formulated question of sociologist Barry Wellman effectively captures this point, "Which types of ties and networks give what kinds of social support?"[10]

Indeed, the discipline of sociology is replete with important research findings and theoretical arguments emphasizing the diverging causal impact of different types of social relations. Let us briefly take up several examples before we return to the empirical analysis underpinning this book's argument. Informal social ties, long of interest to sociologists, are usually included among the alleged components of "social capital" along with formal group memberships and other indicators. However, it is not at all clear how we should weigh different types of informal social ties in constructing a summary measure of "social capital." Let us first address Mark Granovetter's now classic distinction between strong ties (among family members or close friends) and weak ties (among acquaintances or distant friends). In his seminal 1974 study *Getting a Job* and in his more recent review of subsequent research findings, published as an afterword to the 1995 second edition of that study, Granovetter contends that strong ties are especially important for unemployed workers in need of basic, if relatively undesirable, employment, whereas weak ties are typically more useful for employed professionals wishing to secure an improved job at higher pay. Moreover, as Portes and others have noted, the causal impact of strong (and weak) ties may vary from one setting to another; in some settings, strong ties may detract from effective economic performance.[11] The distinction between strong and weak ties—crucial for causal analysis in economic sociology—is masked by the effort to generate one overall summary measure of "social capital."

Crucial distinctions can also be found in the sphere of formal associational involvement. One telling instance can be found in sociology's origins in Emile Durkheim's *Suicide*. Durkheim insists that religious denominations are unlike one another in the extent to which they tightly incorporate members into group life or, alternatively, leave members largely to their own devices as individuals. Tightly integrated groups, in Durkheim's analysis, generate fundamentally different outcomes from weakly integrated groups. More recent scholarship tends to support this classic argument.[12] Thus it is not sufficient to ascertain the prevalence in numbers of associational membership, as is common in quantitative studies of "social capital." If we are serious about social science explanation, we need to know something about the character of the associations to which people belong. Recent important work by Theda Skocpol and Robert Wuthnow underscores the enormous difference in forms of involvement that can be found below the surface of aggregate data on associational membership.[13] If in the search for one overarching measure of "social capital" we lose the ability to distinguish between types of associational life, we end up burying crucial scholarly advances in the sociological tradition.

Another fundamental distinction involves the difference between socially based understandings, such as trust, on the one hand, and social relations including both associational membership and informal ties, on the other hand. In his highly stimulating analysis of "social capital" in Britain, Peter Hall asserts that the overall level of "social capital" in that country has remained quite high, despite the considerable decline in social trust, which he nonetheless takes to represent one component of that overall level.[14] Hall relies largely on measures of associational membership for his claim that "social capital" has remained high. Recent important research on the United States also demonstrates the existence of major differences in the pattern or trajectory of evolution over time among various indicators or understandings of social capital.[15] Yet even in the absence of a formalized summary index, the concept, perhaps because of its rooting in the metaphor offered by economic capital, encourages social scientists to search for an "overall level." Students of "social capital" differ enormously among themselves in the relative weight they place on trust attitudes or on social relations. Thus political scientists Mariano Torcal and José Ramón Montero review data on both formal associational membership and interpersonal trust in Spain, but they emphasize trust attitudes as the most fundamental component of "social capital."[16] The contributions of Hall and others show clearly that these two alleged components of "social capital" need not vary together. The complex and important relationship between trust and tangible social relations is potentially hidden by the search for a summary measure alleged to accurately represent both of these features of social life. The relationship between trust and (specific types of) social relations needs to be studied and not assumed on conceptual grounds. For this relationship to be studied, we need to continue to conceive of trust attitudes and social relations as separate phenomena.

Given that the alleged components of "social capital" can act causally in very different ways producing different outcomes, and need not vary together, the case for building one summary measure of causally relevant social relations is further weakened. To these observations we must add the fact that the so-called components of "social capital" cannot be exchanged for one another. Thus I conclude that the various facets of social life studied under this heading should not be seen to constitute a meaningful whole.

Do Social Relations Represent an Instrumental Investment?

The metaphor of capital, when applied to social life, may encourage the assumption that all causally significant social relations represent investments, much like economic capital, that are instrumentally constructed and deployed for the benefit of the actors involved.[17] Coleman, in his seminal theoretical work on the concept, explicitly rejects the view that "social capital" must necessarily be constructed through the instrumental investment of actors in their social relations. Nonetheless, the instrumentalist view of "social capital" is found in many works on the concept, and the simple linguistic fact that the term *capital* is typically understood to represent an investment by instrumental actors tends to reinforce this position—so long as the debate over the motivational underpinnings of social relations takes place on the terminological terrain of "social capital." As James Baron and Michael Hannon note in their highly useful review of "The Impact of Economics on Contemporary Sociology," there is little point in conceiving of social relations as "social capital" if they are not understood to represent instrumental and investment-like behavior. Baron and Hannon argue that

> unless a characteristic is regarded as an investment for which there is a capital market and an opportunity cost, we fail to see the value of calling it a type of capital, and we are therefore somewhat baffled that sociologists have begun referring to virtually every feature of social life as a form of capital. To the extent that individuals acquire various characteristics virtually automatically through their upbringing or normal social interaction, involving little or no opportunity costs (for them or their parents), we cannot see what is gained by viewing these outcomes as types of social or cultural capital.[18]

In the time since Baron and Hannon published that critical assessment, the "social capital" wave has grown enormously larger, but their critique stands out as one of the most compelling commentaries on the concept. As they suggest, the causal impact of social relations is quite independent of the instrumental energy applied in constructing those relations. My own research findings, reported in the next chapter, show that the causal impact of worker–intellectual ties operates *independently* of any instrumental effort to build the ties. Actual research findings, theoretical analysis, and simple common sense all indicate that the capacity of social ties to shape human outcomes need not be a function of the instrumental calculations present—or absent—in the genesis of those ties. What is the problem, then? The metaphor of capital, if adopted as the primary conceptual perspective for studying the causal impact of social relations, tends to push us constantly toward the search for an instrumentalist understanding of all social life. Given the strong evidence against an *exclusively* instrumentalist perspective on all social life, as long as the study of social relations is largely carried out under the conceptual heading of "social capital," we are likely condemned to an endless and often fruitless debate between advocates and critics of an instrumentalist-only analysis of social relations.

Is There Still Value in This Concept?

Readers will surely differ among themselves in how they assess the criticisms of this currently influential concept I have presented. Assuming, at least for the moment, that one accepts my conceptual argument, does this imply that the notion of social capital lacks any usefulness as a way of framing much social science work? It is undeniably the case that many of the best minds in the social sciences have devoted enormous time and energy to work within this (relatively recent) tradition, leading to many important contributions. Yet if my argument is sound, it may well be that with the benefit of a different conceptual underpinning such contributions would have been substantially greater. I suggest below two general thoughts and one test relevant for assessing the usefulness of the social capital concept.

My critique leaves open the possibility, at least in theory, that the notion of social capital could prove useful as a suggestive, if rather loose, metaphor for understanding the causal impact of social relations. By thinking of social relations as roughly equivalent to economic capital in their ability to facilitate actors' successful pursuit of myriad objectives, we underscore the enormous causal significance of social ties and assert, in a sense, that fundamentally sociological variables are as powerful as conventionally economic ones in the endeavors of individuals and groups. Yet this possible minimalist understanding of "social capital" poses new questions: Is it possible to contain the use of the term to this minimalist metaphor-only version? Can we effectively use the notion of social capital only as a loose metaphor, avoiding the counterproductive tendency to think of it as a measurable variable encompassing many separate components? I am inclined to answer both questions in the negative, but future social science practice will provide the only truly meaningful answer. There is one powerful reason why it would be difficult to contain the use of this term to the minimalist, metaphor-only version. The basis of the metaphor lies in a social science concept that is quantifiable, namely, economic capital. By using the metaphor of capital to frame our discussion of social relations, we invite the effort to assign a summary score to actors and social groups just as we might attempt to ascertain the (economic) capital resources of a firm. It is not easy to think of "social capital" as *only* a loose metaphor and *not as* a quantifiable variable, because economic capital itself can be treated as a quantifiable variable. If the term remains in wide use, it probably will continue to be seen as a quantifiable variable that (it is then inappropriately assumed) can be represented in one summary measure.

Another model for how to locate continuing value in the concept can be found in a type of institutional, or neo-institutional, analysis currently common in political science (and political sociology). Neo-institutionalism, at least in a version common in the field of comparative political science (which is only one of several "new institutionalisms"), offers us a way of examining *contrasts and differences*. Institutions are studied not because they are all the same but because they are different. The contrasts between different institutional forms and practices can help explain meaningfully different outcomes. Institutional analysis of this variety is about presidentialism versus parliamentarism, proportional representation versus single-member districts, centralized national bargaining versus enterprise-level bargaining, regime actors versus state actors, and so forth.[19] But it was not always so. The hugely influential and elegantly argued book of Samuel Huntington, *Political Order in Changing Societies*, made the case for a form of institutional analysis that did formulate an assessment of the overall level of "institutionalization" or institutional strength for each political system. For Huntington, the crucial question involved the *overall level or amount* of institutionalization in a political system rather than the specific type or design of the polity's institutions. This argument led him to mistakenly equate the Soviet Union and the United States in that book's opening passages, and failed to identify many of the questions that would later animate institutional analysts, but the argument's impact at the time was nonetheless enormous.[20]

Can social capital analysis be transformed in a manner similar to that found within comparative institutional analysis by focusing on differences among *types* of social relations (and understandings) instead of on the search for one overarching summary measure of the total amount of "social capital"? Many fine social scientists would like to do just this, and the literature on "social capital" offers numerous suggestive distinctions. Nonetheless, I am not optimistic about the viability of this path if the term "social capital" retains its current heavy usage. The institutional analysis of politics intrinsically pushes us to focus on *particular* institutions and institutional forms. The contrasts among institutional forms are unavoidable because they constitute much of the substance of political debate and mobilization. Constitution makers, the drafters of party or union statutes, the designers and advocates of new public policies—all address issues of institutional *differences*. The world itself constantly forces us to examine and reflect on the meaning of contrasting institutional forms.

By adopting the metaphor of capital as the framework for studying social life, we subject ourselves to very different pressures rooted both in the empirical world and in the structure of the social sciences. We subject ourselves to pressures to uncover the best way to measure the overall amount of "social capital" in meaningful units. Given that economic capital can be so measured, why aren't we able to do the same with "social capital"? To put the matter only slightly differently, we increase the risk of conceiving of all social relations as basically similar—even if our empirical studies emphatically tell us otherwise. Moreover, by embracing the terminology of economic capital for the study of society, we subject ourselves to the tendency to view all social relations as instrumentally based, even though that assumption is valid for only some causally meaningful social relations, not for all such relations. We are pushed toward a search for an overall summary amount of social connectedness and away from the useful examination of causally meaningful differences.

Assessing the Usefulness of "Social Capital" Measures in Empirical Analysis

Perhaps the most appropriate test of the usefulness of the "social capital" approach in causal explanation lies in empirical analysis itself. Every causal argument emphasizing the role of "social capital" ought to be able to contend with the competing claim that *specific forms of social relations or social attitudes* could offer more explanatory power and clarity than could a *general summary measure* of the overarching concept. This is, after all, an issue taken up at considerable length—albeit from the reverse perspective—in this chapter. To restate the point quite directly, social scientists face a fundamental choice in causal analysis: Do we explain variations in the world best by focusing on the impact of specific types of social relations (and/or trust-like attitudes), or by examining the generalized impact of a summary measure intended to capture the overall essence of "social capital"? On the basis of our own data, we cannot resolve the issue for all conceivable uses of the social capital concept, but we can offer a straightforward approach to settle the matter for the phenomena of concern to us in this book, an approach that can easily be applied to many other concrete issues.

The data offer us three variables highly relevant for assessing the possibility that an overarching measure of "social capital" might provide a better explanation for globalizing discursive horizons than do the social ties on which we focus. I do not attempt to formulate a summary index of these three variables. In the absence of a universally accepted solution to the challenge of operationalization, I prefer to examine these three alternatives to determine which among them offers the greatest explanatory promise. We will select the most powerful of the three alternatives and then incorporate it into a multivariate model intended to systematically weigh the relative explanatory significance of competing explanations for the differences we have observed in discursive horizons.

The three variables we shall examine are *total organizations*, which simply quantifies the number of organizations that each respondent reported to exist locally; *useful organizations*, which does the same for one subset of that overall set of locally present organizations, namely, those that respondents report to be useful in pursuing collective objectives; and the *collective efforts index*, which sums the responses of the interviewed leaders to ten items that ask about the prevalence of collective efforts within the locality in pursuit of various objectives such as cultural activity, economic development, local festivals, supporting local sports teams, political endeavors, and so forth. To specify further, this last variable, the collective efforts index, measures the respondents' perceptions of the level of collective energy deployed locally in pursuit of ten different types of objectives.

All three variables have a plausible claim to the attention of those taken—or at least intrigued—by the notion of social capital. A long tradition in the social sciences—firmly rooted in the work of Tocqueville, and thus prior to the recent theoretical discussions examined here—emphasizes the relevance of formal organizations for the ability of individuals to act collectively and more broadly for the vitality of democracy. Indeed this classic tradition has been a contributing influence in the development of the "social capital" school, many of whose members emphasize strongly the special importance

TABLE 4.1
Social capital variables in explanatory comparison through logistic regression
(logistic regression coefficients, with standard errors in parentheses)

Independent Variables	Useful Organizations	Total Organizations
Useful organizations	.19*	N/a
	(.10)	
Total organizations	N/a	.07
		(.07)
Collective efforts index	−.08	−.07
	(.17)	(.17)
Constant	−.52	−.32
	(.55)	(.56)
N	299	299

* $p < .10$

Note: To test the relationship between the social capital variables and respondents'
disposition toward a globalizing discourse, we regressed social capital variables of interest on the
dependent variable (1 = globalizing discourse; 0 = otherwise), using logistic regression. Both
regression models included the collective efforts index; the first model included the indicator for
useful organizations, and the second model included the indicator for total organizations. Results
show that only the variable for useful organizations reaches marginal significance at $p = .07$;
the other indicator did not come close to significance. Further examination of the pairwise
correlations between these variables reveals that only "useful organizations" is correlated with
globalizing discourse at or near significance ($p = .07$). N/a, not applicable.

of formal organizations for the broader phenomenon they conceptu-
alize. The variable *total organizations* offers us a straightforward
way to measure the presence of organizations. One could contend,
nonetheless, that *useful organizations* more closely captures the
spirit of much work in this theoretical school, including the formulation by James Coleman. After all, Coleman insists that only those
social relations that prove *useful* to actors in pursuit of their objectives should be understood to form "social capital." Thus we shall
examine both measures of organizational presence. Finally, the collective efforts index measures the overall propensity of local residents
to act collectively, at least in the perception of those interviewed. If
there genuinely is an overall amount of "social capital" characterizing localities as such, this should be reflected in the localities' higher
or lower propensity toward collective endeavors. This variable can
thus plausibly be construed as a marker of the *expected effects* of
"social capital." Given how difficult it is to specify a comprehensive
list of the *components* of "social capital," it is not an unreasonable
strategy to instead measure the overall expected effects. If "social

capital" theory is well grounded, these overall effects should be a reliable indicator of the prior strength of this difficult-to-measure social property. In this sense, we can conceive of the collective efforts index as a "shadow variable" capturing the effects, or the force, of a phenomenon alleged to exist. If "social capital" represents a meaningful "whole," then we should be able to clearly discern the shadow (or "glow") it casts by focusing on the overall propensity for collective action within a community.

We shall now assess the relative ability of these three variables to contribute to explaining variations in democracy's public rhetorics. Because the variable I want to account for—the propensity to articulate globalizing discursive horizons—is a dichotomy, I employ logistic regression analysis, the data analysis technique I use in the next chapter when concluding the overall effort to assess competing explanations. I report here two logistic models, one with total organizations and the other with useful organizations, two variables with an intercorrelation too high for them to be included simultaneously. Both models include the collective efforts index. As the data reported in table 4.1 show, *useful organizations* clearly emerges as the strongest of these three variables. In statistical terms, this variable attains significance only at the rather loose .10 level. The other two variables fail to attain significance even at the .15 level. Strikingly, the collective efforts index exerts no meaningful predictive effect on globalizing discursive horizons in this analysis. Thus we find no evidence that a generalized measure of the presumed effects of "social capital" can help account for discursive horizons. These findings seem to counsel considerable skepticism about the ability of "social capital" to displace intellectual–worker ties as the best explanation for variations in discursive horizons and thus in the quality of democratic life. Nonetheless, one of the "social capital" variables appears to merit inclusion in a more complete multivariate model, even if only to test its explanatory power against that of our central variable, the strength of (intellectual–worker) social ties, and other competing explanatory variables. It is to this broader analysis assessing various competing explanations that we now turn.

5 Pursuing Alternative Explanations

Our analysis of social ties and discursive horizons in chapter 3 clearly established an empirical association between these two phenomena—an association that attains considerable strength under certain circumstances, and above all within certain subcultural contexts. The empirical findings we have reviewed are at a minimum suggestive, but the interpretation here advanced must still be subjected to the test of alternative causal explanations. Only by seriously examining the possibility that this book's argument is misplaced can we gain confidence that social ties do indeed represent a powerful determinant of democracy's rhetorics. We cannot examine every possible hypothesis that might conceivably occur to an intelligent critic—given the theoretically infinite number of alternative explanations one might propose—but we can explore several major alternative explanations, all of them sufficiently plausible to merit attention.[1] The possibilities we analyze in this chapter vary substantially in their conceptual breadth and import, but all of them represent reasonable hypotheses that we can address through the available data.

The alternative explanations we examine largely fall into several general categories. The first and most direct explanatory challenge we take up poses the issue of where one should search for the determinants of local communities' discursive horizons. Perhaps we have misplaced our explanatory efforts and would have been better advised to examine the impact of macropolitical factors such as national institutions, organizations, and leaders on the rhetorics articulated in our forty-nine communities. The second and the simplest set of possibilities focuses on social characteristics and collective experiences of the interviewed leaders that might conceivably shape their discursive horizons. Under this general heading, we will review the impact of educational attainment and of opposition to the Franco regime on the globalizing discursive horizons we emphasize.

The third alternative explanation we contemplate involves the unavoidable question of causal direction and related issues involving a possible unmeasured prior variable underlying the entire ties-to-rhetoric dynamic: Could it be that globalizing discursive horizons encourage leaders to seek out and build ties to intellectuals rather than the reverse? Or perhaps the instrumental calculations of some leaders and/or their political sensibilities encourage them both to construct ties to intellectuals and to articulate their agendas through globalizing rhetorics. Although logically distinct from one another, in this case the hypotheses of reverse causation and of a prior unmeasured variable are strongly interrelated. To state the matter quite directly, Do the ties actually cause (or influence) the form taken by discursive horizons, or do leaders' public discourses—or prior causal variables such as the leaders' political strategies and sensibilities—instead help to generate the social ties? After all, it seems highly plausible to argue that local leaders who search for connections between their locality and extralocal phenomena in both their policy proposals and political rhetoric might also, as a result, be inclined to pursue ties with intellectuals. Social interchanges and conversations between workers and intellectuals could be the result—and not the cause—of the political tendency to draw connections between the specific and the general. The final competing explanations we must contemplate offer alternative conceptualizations of the social relations, or social contexts, that shape discursive horizons. We reviewed this issue in some conceptual depth in the preceding chapter, but we must now examine empirical evidence on this point.

Placing the Action: Locally Based Social Relations or National Actors and Institutions

A critic of this book's argument might well allege that I have fundamentally misplaced the action: Is it not possible that the primary explanation for globalizing discursive horizons lies not in the locally based social relations of working-class leaders but instead in the (greater or lesser) ability of national political institutions and leaders to sway local actors to formulate their concerns in a language transcending locality? Indeed many outstanding political scientists would doubtless prefer to interpret globalizing discursive horizons as the result of strong national institutions (including parties) or compelling national leaders. National elites and institutions surely deserve much analytical attention, but whether they can account for variations in the phenomenon we seek to understand—the political discourse generated by local communities—is an empirical question to which our data speak quite directly.

The question of where best to focus explanatory efforts, at the macropolitical or the local community level, connects directly with a now classic issue in political and social theory. For well over one hundred years, a fundamental concern of influential students of democracy has centered on the ability of local communities and critical individuals to formulate and express their ideas with independence from powerful external actors such as the central state. This is perhaps the most basic preoccupation of Alexis de Tocqueville in *Democracy in America*. For Tocqueville, liberty—understood to be reflected in the free and lively interchange of ideas—is guaranteed in a democratic society only if local communities (as well as associations, both civil and political in nature) maintain the ability to formulate and communicate ideas that challenge powerful political actors and structures as well as majority opinion. In drafting the questionnaire for the survey work underpinning this study, I set out to capture, as best as possible, the interviewed leaders' perspective on the Tocquevillean question of local political autonomy in formulating and communicating political arguments. Respondents were asked to choose between the following two sentences:

> As much as one might like to develop strategies and proposals at the local level, the truth is that in order to join forces with others it is a good idea to adjust local actions to the initiatives and strategies agreed upon by progressive forces in other similar municipalities and at the national level.

> As much as one might like to take into account what is being done in other similar localities and at the national level, the personality and the decision-making ability of this locality or its immediate vicinity make it important for our political and union activities to be based in large measure on our perspectives and experiences.

This questionnaire item only partially captures the full complexity and the sheer breadth of Tocqueville's enduring perspective on democratic liberty and local political autonomy, but nonetheless the survey question does allow us to discriminate clearly between leaders who tend to defer to external political actors and others who resist guidance from extralocal forces, preferring instead to formulate political initiatives and strategies on their own at the local level. On the face of it, it might be reasonable to expect advocates of local autonomy to articulate their programs in the language of defensive localism. By the same token, we might well expect globalizing discursive horizons to predominate among those who defer to the cue provided by national-level political forces. There would be a neat and simple logic to the data if the extralocal points of reference reflected in globalizing discursive horizons were most often employed by local leaders who base their political arguments on input received from national political forces. If such expectations were supported by the data, we would have to conclude that despite the affection one might feel for those Tocquevillean heroes who uphold the principle of local autonomy in political debate and public discussion, the roots of globalizing discursive horizons lie outside the local level in the ability of national institutions and leaders to shape the political agenda of local leaders. We would then be best advised to focus our explanatory efforts almost exclusively on the preferred terrain of so many excellent political scientists: national political institutions, such as parties, and national political (or opinion) elites.

Despite the seeming logic of this perspective, the survey data offer no support for the critical assertion that we have misplaced the action by focusing on locally based social relations. As the data in figure 5.1 show, discursive horizons are not strongly related to the respondents' choice between local autonomy or guidance from outside the locality in formulating political arguments. Indeed, the Tocquevillean heroes who defend local autonomy are slightly more likely to embrace globalizing discursive horizons than those preferring to follow the political lead of external actors. The difference is not great in magnitude: among proponents of local autonomy in elaborating political endeavors, 45.9% prefer globalizing discursive horizons, whereas among those who rely instead on outside influence when formulating political initiatives, a somewhat smaller proportion, 38.3%, manifests the tendency to articulate political claims through globalizing rhetorics.

In case there had been any doubt on the point, the data underscore that national political organizations such as unions and parties influence activities and debate in numerous local communities: many

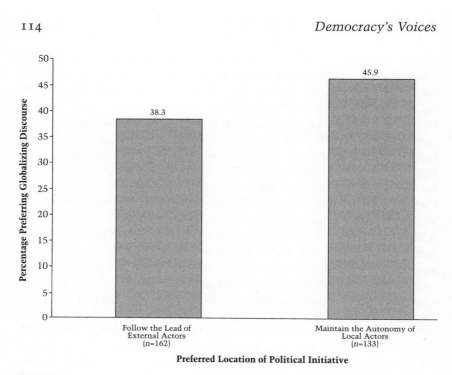

Preferred Location of Political Initiative

FIG. 5.1
Globalizing discursive horizons by preferred location of political initiative. The relationship is not statistically significant.

leaders do indeed defer to political "lines," programs, and endeavors that emerge from outside their localities. Yet this dynamic is only *one* of the patterns reflected in the data. It is equally clear that in the Spanish case here examined, much of the energy and direction of politics arises more or less *autonomously* from local communities—a pattern that Tocqueville argued was typical of the United States. This largely independent contribution to political life, wherever it may be found, can take the form of broadly posed objectives and analyses articulated through globalizing rhetorics, or alternatively, this independent contribution can take the simple form of defensive localism. But to the extent that local political autonomy shapes discursive horizons, it appears to actually encourage, even if only slightly, globalizing rhetorics, whereas the formative influence of national political institutions appears paradoxically likely to favor defensive localism in the communities I have studied.[2] We shall explore this issue more fully in the context of multivariate analysis later in the chapter. For now we can conclude that the effect of this variable seems to be quite weak, thus requiring us to look elsewhere for explanation.

The data on the Tocquevillean question clearly suggest that the roots of globalizing rhetorics often lie in locally based phenomena of some sort rather than in an alleged inclination to follow national elites or to mechanically accept the discipline of national political organizations. Thus the effort to look beyond the unmistakable import of national political institutions and this book's emphasis on social relations such as the ties between workers and intellectuals stand on strong ground. This book's argument is not intended to provide a fully exhaustive explanation for all settings in which globalizing discursive horizons characterize political life. The more modest effort here is to build the case that locally based social ties strongly impact the shape of political discourse in democracy. The causal relevance of national political institutions is not in any sense negated by this argument, but by the same token my findings do show that the causal relevance of macrolevel institutions is not so great as to eclipse the power of individuals' (often extra-institutional) social ties to remake public rhetorics. Much of the action determining how communities engage in politics will evade those researchers whose explanatory focus rests *exclusively* on the terrain of nationwide parties, unions, and national political elites. My argument does not seek to challenge the enormous usefulness of macrolevel institutional analysis—unless such institutions are taken as the exclusive mechanism through which social processes shape politics. This conclusion leaves unresolved one intriguing question concerning the role of institutions: What is the relative impact of differing national political institutions on the discursive horizons of local leaders? We have interviewed municipal-level leaders in the principal unions and (labor-oriented) parties of Spain's industrial communities, and thus it is appropriate to ask whether these organizations exert differing effects on the rhetorics of their local leaders. I leave this important question for the multivariate analysis taken up later in the chapter.

Internal Theorists or Intellectuals and the Nature of Social Ties: Two Additional Possibilities

Two additional possibilities, both of them involving the decision of where to locate major explanatory efforts, deserve attention: the

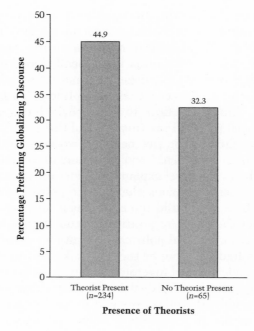

FIG. 5.2
Globalizing discursive horizons by the presence of theorists. A Fisher's exact test of relationship between the presence of internal theorists and the tendency toward a globalizing discourse reveals marginal significance at $p = .09$ (two-tailed test) and $p = .05$ (one-tailed test).

role of theorists internal to the labor movement and the relative explanatory impact of different types of social ties. One might hypothesize that in the search for social underpinnings of globalizing discourse, it is the presence of reflective and theoretically oriented individuals within the ranks of labor that matters more than ties to external intellectuals. The now classic Gramscian conception of organic intellectuals could be seen to support this line of analysis. Thus it was absolutely essential to ask the working-class leaders we interviewed about the presence of such internal "theorists." A large majority of the respondents, just over three-quarters of the total sample, replied affirmatively, noting the presence of theorists within their local political world.

To what degree does the presence of theorists within the local political world of working-class leaders help to generate globalizing discursive horizons? As the data reported in figure 5.2 show, global discursive horizons are indeed more prevalent where internal theorists are present. The strength of the effect appears marginally weaker than that of ties to (generally external) intellectuals in the simple bivariate analysis. We clearly need to turn to multivariate analysis, as we shall do in the final section of this chapter, to sort out the relative causal impact of internal theorists and ties to external intellectuals. Only through such analysis can the explanatory contribution to be made by the Gramscian focus on internal theorists be determined.

Another intriguing avenue of analysis is to explore the explanatory impact of different types of ties. The data on worker–intellectual connections make it possible to distinguish between ties that were described as including some component of friendship (or friendly informal interchange) as opposed to those ties that were exclusively institutional in nature, lacking any informal or friendship component. I call these two categories of interaction *friendship ties* and *institutional ties only*. The friendship ties often included a major institutional component—in the internal workings of a political party, for example. I have included in the friendship ties category all connections involving at least some friendship or friendly informal component. As the data reported in figure 5.3 show, the type of tie seems unrelated to its effect. Institutions, in our analysis, are crucially important in helping to provide the setting for the development of most intellectual–worker ties, and purely institutional ties seem *as likely* to foster globalizing discourse as friendship ties. Yet some ties emerge outside institutions, and friendship ties (which may have emerged within or outside institutions) seem roughly as effective as purely institutional ties in the underpinning of globalizing rhetorics. The findings thus far, which need to be carefully examined and refined in multivariate analysis, suggest that the connections between institutions, social ties, and public rhetorics are quite complex. Institutions play an enormously important role in building social connections, but ultimately for *some* questions it is those connections, regardless of where they emerge, that matter more than the institutions themselves.[3]

Social Background and Discursive Horizons

The social background of local leaders must influence, in some measure, the rhetorics they articulate, unless the fundamental assumptions of most sociological research are strangely inapplicable

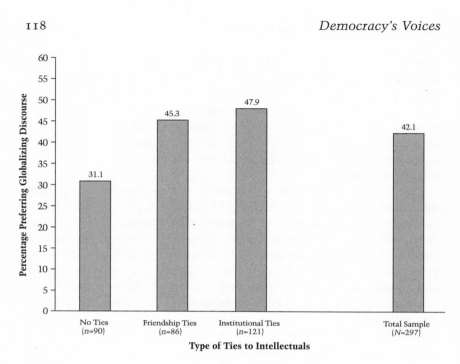

FIG. 5.3
Globalizing discursive horizons by the type of ties. When those without ties are
removed, the relationship between the type of tie and those preferring a globalizing
discourse is not significant $(p = .71; n = 207)$.

to the terrain we examine. For us, the most important question is
whether social background and experience exert a causal impact on
public discourse so strong, once we stop to take careful note of it,
that the significance of social ties fades or even disappears: When we
incorporate in the analysis the explanatory weight of social background, do social ties continue to demonstrate an ability to shape
democracy's public life? To answer this question we will examine
two social experiences likely to shape leaders' rhetorics, one a historically salient collective experience and the other a standard marker
of individual achievement. The collective experience we analyze is
participation in the anti-Franco opposition movement during the
long decades of authoritarian repression.[4] The individual marker of
achievement we examine is the impact of educational attainment on
leaders' public discourse.

Nearly two-thirds of the local leaders interviewed affirm that they participated in the opposition movement during the authoritarian period, which led often to arrest and in some instances to prolonged imprisonment.[5] There are several reasons why veterans of the democratic resistance to authoritarian repression might be especially inclined to articulate globalizing discourses. During the Franco period, labor's defense of specific worker interests almost invariably required the use of illegal tactics—given the comprehensive restrictions then imposed on political and union activity—and thus struggles that began as defensive local endeavors of a limited sort frequently assumed a far broader significance. When local strikes and protests encountered the regime's repression, they quickly turned into a testing ground between the forces of authoritarianism and democracy. The historical experience of workers and their organized advocates under Francoism was far more complex than a telegraphic summary can adequately communicate, but the tendency of many local struggles to end up posing the general issue of democratic freedom is a clear feature of the period. Thus the difficult challenge posed by resisting dictatorship led many opposition activists at least at the time to draw deeply compelling connections between local problems and larger issues.

How does this historical experience of participation in the anti-Franco opposition influence the discursive horizons of today's local leaders? Does the tendency to connect the meaning of local struggles to large-scale issues persist among those who were pressed by circumstances to do so in the context of authoritarian rule, or has the impact of that historical experience largely vanished in the years intervening between the end of Francoist repression and the time of my field research? As the data in figure 5.4 show, veterans of the opposition movement remain substantially more likely than their counterparts without such an experience to defend their political agendas through globalizing rhetorics. Among the veterans of the opposition experience, nearly half, 48.2%, prefer globalizing discursive horizons, whereas among the leaders without such an experience approximately one-third, 32.1%, are inclined toward globalizing rhetorics. Unlike social ties, the opposition experience actually exerts its strongest impact on discourse within the socialist subculture, where, as the data in figure 5.5 show, the tendency to embrace global discursive horizons reaches 53.7% of the leaders among the veterans of the opposition as opposed to 27.3% among those without

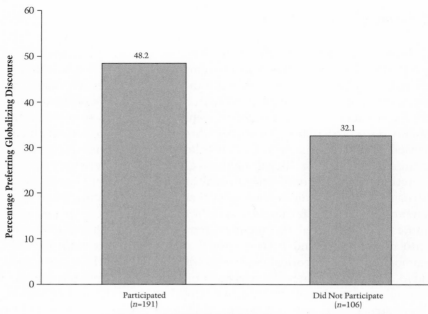

FIG. 5.4
Globalizing discursive horizons by participation in political opposition to the Franco regime. Pearson's chi-square tests reveal that the relationship is significant at $p = .01$.

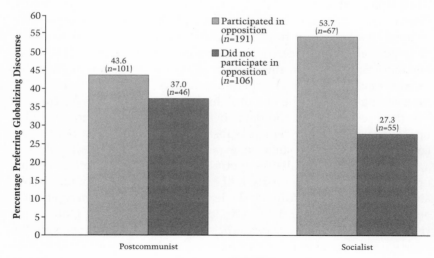

FIG. 5.5
Globalizing discursive horizons by participation in political opposition to the Franco regime for the two subcultures. When the relationship between globalizing discourse and participation in the anti-Franco movement is tested separately for each subculture, the results reveal substantial statistical significance ($p = .01$) only in the socialist subculture.

such an experience. The extraordinary strength of this effect in the socialist subculture poses an interesting question we must leave for the next chapter, when we carefully examine contrasts between the two subcultures. In the postcommunist subculture as well, the opposition veterans are those most likely to speak in globalizing discourses, but the effect is substantially weaker (and lacks statistical significance). In chapter 6 we explore more fully this and other disparities between the subcultures. The historical effort to actively oppose authoritarian repression has retained, for those who participated, a powerful ability to shape their sense of politics and public life.

How does the collective experience of actively opposing authoritarianism interact with social ties in shaping discursive horizons? Does the inclusion of this shared historical experience reduce or eliminate the causal force of worker–intellectual linkages in this analysis? Before we examine the data, it is important to note one crucial, if rather obvious, point: the opposition movement is a *historically closed* episode no longer able to attract new participants. All oppositional involvement took place, by definition, before the return of democratic freedoms during 1977. Thus the ability of that movement to *directly* shape the political sensibilities of leaders and activists must inevitably decline over time, as opposition veterans are replaced in their positions of leadership by others, many of them too young to have been involved in the anti-Franco movement. If, in causal analysis, the influence of the opposition movement thoroughly overpowers the impact of social ties on discursive horizons, then the globalizing rhetorics here emphasized are virtually condemned to a historical process of steady erosion and decline. Globalizing discursive horizons will prove to be a sustainable feature of local political life only if ongoing current-day features of social life encourage such rhetorics.

The data reported in figure 5.6 offer strong indications that a steady historical erosion of globalizing rhetorics is not inevitable, precisely because the causal power of social ties largely compensates for the absence of an oppositional experience among many leaders. Among opposition participants, with their historically given predisposition toward globalizing discursive horizons, worker–intellectual ties exert a causal impact substantially smaller than in the sample as a whole: the increment in globalizing discourse afforded by multiple ties is only 11.7% when contrasted to those with no ties. Even without the

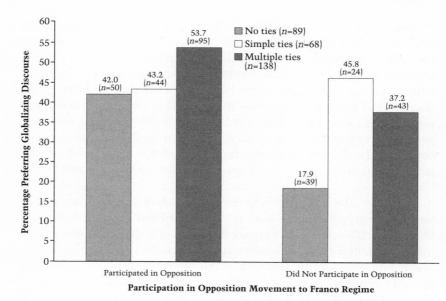

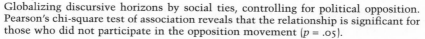

FIG. 5.6
Globalizing discursive horizons by social ties, controlling for political opposition.
Pearson's chi-square test of association reveals that the relationship is significant for
those who did not participate in the opposition movement ($p = .05$).

benefit of ties to intellectuals, opposition veterans often embrace
globalizing rhetorics; social ties enhance this initially favorable
predisposition only to a small extent.

Among leaders without any experience in the opposition, however,
the impact of social ties is large, generating a greater than twofold
increase in the predisposition to adopt globalizing discourse. *Thus
social ties play their greatest causal role among those whom history
has rendered otherwise least likely to draw globalizing discursive
connections.* Through the generative power of social ties to remake
public discourse, the empty space left by the slow erosion of the
direct oppositional experience is partially overcome. Yet, like so
many empty spaces left by the passing of historical time, this one is
only imperfectly filled. The social ties I emphasize are powerful in
their impact on public life, but they cannot fully take the place of
the historically closed contribution to public life offered by the veterans of the anti-Franco movement. Our data suggest that when the

opposition generation has passed entirely from the scene, globalizing discursive horizons will likely be somewhat less prevalent than they are today, especially in the socialist subculture—unless a new collective historical experience or new movements regenerate the desire to draw connections between the particular and the general, the local and the translocal. By the same token, a new flourishing of boundary-crossing social ties could conceivably compensate for the passing from the scene of opposition veterans. Distinctive generational experiences, as numerous scholars have argued, may powerfully shape social and political life, as in the case of the American World War II generation, whose major contribution to civic involvement Robert Putnam has recently championed.[6] Significantly, our data show that locally based social ties can largely (although not fully) compensate for the empty space left by the time-bound closing of a decisive historical episode such as Spain's anti-Franco opposition movement.

Fundamentally different is the effect on discourse of disparate levels of educational attainment. There are several reasons why education might help encourage relatively complex forms of political argument characterized by their globalizing discursive horizons. Education not only transmits specific knowledge but, quite obviously, also encourages the development of verbal and interpretive skills, just as it diffuses cultural understandings predominant among the educators. Skills, knowledge, and cultural assumptions acquired by local leaders during their schooling could all enhance their predisposition to draw connections in their public rhetoric between the local and the translocal, the concrete and the abstract. Assuming that education plays this causal role, the effect could be *continuous and linear*— with the prevalence of globalizing rhetorics increasing steadily in conjunction with incrementally higher levels of schooling—or it could be *qualitative*, with an increase in globalizing rhetorics taking place rather abruptly once a meaningful threshold is crossed.

I examine the effects of education by dividing the respondents into four categories: those with a primary education or none at all; those with a middle school education (the minimal level required by educational policy until a reform that arrived too late to affect respondents in this survey); those with a high school education (designed to prepare students for subsequent university-level education); and those with at least some university education. I have included in each of these four categories persons who began but did not complete studies at that level. Our empirical findings suggest that education

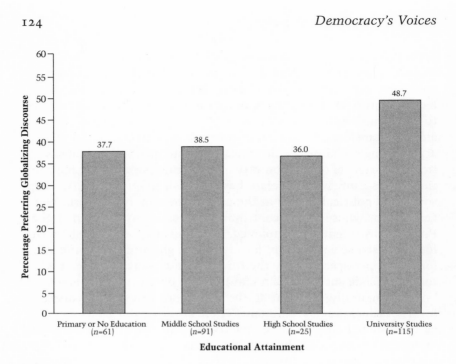

FIG. 5.7
Globalizing discursive horizons by educational attainment. When a linear-by-linear test of association is used, relationship nears significance at $p = .11$. Additionally, a dummy variable coding of college tested against a globalizing discourse is marginally significant at $p = .07$.

does indeed exert some causal influence on discursive horizons and that the effect takes the form of a qualitative difference between university-level higher education and all other levels of educational attainment. As the data in figure 5.7 show, the proportion of those leaders who embrace globalizing discursive horizons is virtually identical among the three educational categories below that of university studies. Among local leaders with higher, or university-level, education, with its transmission of many types of complex knowledge and cultural understanding, the predisposition to speak in globalizing rhetorics increases by just over 10%. A qualitative change—at least in the probability that individuals will articulate complex political arguments—seems to occur when individuals experience at least some higher education. Thus the bivariate effect of education is fairly clear, rather abrupt, and decidedly moderate in its magnitude.

When this moderate effect of education is introduced into the analysis, does it reduce or even eliminate the causal impact of social ties? One could, after all, hypothesize that leaders with a university-level education are those most likely to build ties to intellectuals; their experiences in the university could well establish network ties to intellectuals that persist after the end of their studies. Even absent such enduring network ties rooted in one's university years, the skills learned at the university could still facilitate the subsequent building of ties to intellectuals. Perhaps higher education is responsible for *both* intellectual–worker ties and globalizing discursive horizons. If so, the causal argument I have developed would be thoroughly mistaken, or spurious. The explanation for both worker–intellectual ties and globalizing discourse would, in this scenario, lie in a prior phenomenon, namely, the university education of some but not all working-class community leaders.

The empirical findings here and in the multivariate analyses reported in the final section of this chapter undercut such a view and thus underscore the substantial causal impact of social ties, even once we take into account educational achievement with its ability to facilitate somewhat the emergence of worker–intellectual ties. As the data in figure 5.8 suggest, in two of the four categories of educational attainment, social ties exert an impact on discursive horizons; in the remaining two educational groups, the effect is at best quite small and thus fails to meet a reasonable standard of statistical significance. The effect reaches its greatest magnitude in the educational categories that encompass the greatest number of respondents: those with university studies (where the effect appears to be dichotomous, differentiating those with ties from those without) and those with studies only through the middle school level. In both categories the causal power of social ties manifests itself—and with roughly equal force in the two cases, despite the obvious and large difference between them in purely educational terms. Moreover, the increment in globalizing discursive horizons generated by ties to intellectuals is, within these two educational categories (middle school studies and university-level studies), clearly greater than the increment directly provided by university-level studies in bivariate analysis (as reflected in fig. 5.7). Thus a leader with education only through the middle school level and with multiple ties to intellectuals is substantially more likely to articulate globalizing discursive horizons (46.9%) than is a leader who has studied in a university but who maintains no ties

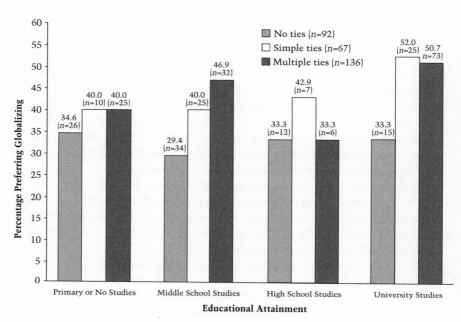

FIG. 5.8
Globalizing discursive horizons by ties to intellectuals, controlling for educational attainment. The relationship nears marginal significance at $p = .14$ only for the middle school studies group.

to intellectuals (33.3%). In the social process shaping a local leader's discursive style, social ties can more than compensate for the lack of an advanced formal education.

We are left with one unavoidable question posed by the data: Why is the effect of social ties on discourse somewhat weaker among members of the remaining two educational categories, those with only a primary school education or less, and those with a high school–level education? It is worth noting that substantially fewer respondents are found in these two educational categories than in the larger groupings within which ties do significantly enhance globalizing rhetorics. Even if all the cases in these two categories are added together, they represent less than 30% of the overall sample. With these relatively small numbers, statistically significant findings are less likely than within larger categories encompassing more individuals. The extremely weak (but still positive) relationship between ties and discourse in the two smaller categories, as reported in the data, could well be smaller than the real relationship in the underlying population, but there is no specific reason to believe this to be the case. It would be unwarranted to wish away this finding by arguing that it is a statistical artifact of the sample. We are better off, instead, focusing on the specific characteristics of each of the four educational categories.

These two smaller categories represent, in a sense, anomalies that depart from the normal pattern of educational attainment. In Spain, up to the time of the survey, education was required through the middle school level. Educational experiences that ended at the primary level represented a vestige from an earlier historical period with inadequate educational facilities in many local areas. Many older workers faced, in their youth, educational opportunities far more limited than those enjoyed by today's Spanish youth, and that historical disadvantage is reflected in these data by the respondents who report educational attainment only through the primary level. High school studies were not required until an educational reform was implemented in 1990, just as this survey was launched, and therefore after the educational experience of the survey respondents had already been set. Thus, high school studies, when they were pursued by the respondents, usually reflected the students' initial intent to continue on to the university level.

These basic features of the educational profile of Spaniards make it possible to offer the following sketch-like characterization of the four groupings: individuals with only primary education (or no formal studies at all) are typically relatively old people from a poor rural background. Those with middle school studies are, in a sense, mainstream working-class individuals who completed the legally required educational sequence and then left school, often for economic reasons. Those with high school studies typically considered the possibility of pursuing higher education but abandoned their studies at the high school level for any one of several possible reasons: economic necessity, academic difficulty, or a simple lack of interest. Those with university-level studies spent at least some time doing university course work, although some did not complete their higher education. Thus we can conclude that where economic circumstances clearly lead teenagers to terminate their studies when they have completed the minimum legal requirement (i.e., among the respondents with a middle school education only), and where

students succeed in at least initiating a university education, social
ties with intellectuals help to shape the discourses of working-class
leaders. Perhaps what is most striking is that, despite the obvious difference between these two groups in educational terms, the magnitude of the effect exerted by social ties is remarkably similar in the
two cases. A higher education is not required for worker–intellectual
ties to remake public discourse.

One additional pattern deserves attention: ties to intellectuals are
especially prevalent among the working-class leaders with a higher
education. Indeed, nearly half the respondents who maintain multiple contacts with intellectuals have had some university-level education. It is largely for this reason that those with higher education
are the most likely to embrace globalizing rhetorics. If we restrict the
analysis to leaders with no ties to intellectuals, those with university-level studies are essentially no more likely to articulate global
discursive horizons than are the other no-tie leaders with lower levels
of educational attainment. Without the benefit of ties to intellectuals, a university-level education would likely leave unchanged a
leader's public voice: the predisposition of highly educated leaders to
articulate their political goals through globalizing discursive horizons
rests heavily on their tendency to build ties to intellectuals. There
are two very different reasons why leaders with higher education may
be especially likely to maintain ties to intellectuals. Their academic
training may well make it easier for them to undertake interchanges
with intellectuals. After all, in the university they have been exposed
regularly to intellectual life and discussion. But there is another fundamentally important reason why these respondents are those most
likely to sustain ties with intellectuals: their personal biographies
have brought them into contact with intellectuals and intellectuals-
to-be during the years of university study. The university represents
only one of many life-course settings in which friendships and social
ties with potential long-lasting significance may emerge. Some of the
ties, initially facilitated by the trajectory of one's personal biography,
erode or disappear over time, but many such ties—clearly rooted in
a particular episode or period of one's life—endure. In this fashion,
some of the ties noted in our study initially emerged during the
leaders' university studies. The simple fact that university graduates
shared, during their years of study, physical spaces, collective efforts,
and other experiences with intellectuals and intellectuals-to-be likely
explains their disproportionate propensity to interact with intellectuals years later while serving as local leaders.

Nonetheless, numerous worker–intellectual ties develop among leaders with lower educational attainment, and thus without the benefit of experiences shared with intellectuals during university study. Ties emerge for many different reasons, including friendship originating in childhood (and sustained through adulthood), joint political endeavors, specific encounters in professional life, and as argued previously, interchanges during university studies. The causal impact of these ties for the two largest educationally defined groups of respondents manifests itself independently of whether the ties' emergence was facilitated by university study on the part of the local leaders. University studies tend to encourage the formation of ties to intellectuals, *but no matter why such ties come into existence, once they emerge they are capable of reshaping democracy's public discourse.* Educational attainment is associated with globalizing discursive horizons because of the social ties engendered by university-level study.

Causal Direction and the Ties' Perceived Utility

One of the most common, and difficult, challenges in causal analysis is to establish firmly the direction of an effect. In this study, the possibility of reverse causation must be taken very seriously indeed, for it is perfectly plausible to suggest that social ties to intellectuals could be the *result* rather than the *cause* of globalizing discourses, or of some highly related underlying variable. Perhaps some leaders' underlying political or cultural frame of mind leads them both to speak in globalizing discursive horizons and to build ties to intellectuals as simply two elements of a general strategy intended to forge political connections. The ties, in this scenario, would follow from a prior inclination to draw connections in discourse and more broadly in political action. Ties would be most appropriately seen as an outcome, not as an explanation. Moreover, by this logic, globalizing discursive horizons should be well within the reach of leaders lacking ties to intellectuals. If the causal reality is indeed the reverse of what I have argued, leaders predisposed to think and speak globally should find the way to do so with relative ease—and even if, for some reason, ties to intellectuals prove difficult to strike up and sustain. Indeed, if a prior predisposition leads to *both* ties and globalizing discourse, then both of these effects should follow fairly easily from that predisposition.

My qualitative findings from extensive interviews with the leaders show instead that the phenomena we have been examining are quite unlikely to be the simple result of a shared underlying predisposition. A number of local leaders noted that it was *difficult* to globalize in their rhetoric—even when they wanted to do so.[7] Perhaps most eloquent on this score was an IU leader in Alcoi who lamented that "the immediacy of problems suffocates us." He went on to explain that it proved quite difficult in practice to articulate globalizing rhetorics. The same IU leader saw, in his political formation's contacts with both intellectuals and unions, the positive influence leading the local IU chapter to emphasize districtwide solutions.[8] Given the intrinsic difficulty of articulating globalizing rhetorics, ties and conversations with intellectuals proved quite helpful to many of those leaders who experienced them. However, the ties themselves should not be seen as equally viable in all contexts. The proximity of the industrial towns to universities and other concentrations of intellectuals varied considerably. Respondents in Puertollano, a medium-sized industrial town in La Mancha, emphasized that both the growth of the nearby university in Ciudad Real and the development of a high-speed rail link to Madrid facilitated contacts with intellectuals, leading to an increase of such connections in Puertollano in the early 1990s.[9]

Neither ties to intellectuals nor globalizing rhetorics appear to follow effortlessly and automatically from an underlying favorable predisposition. Yet suggestive as these qualitative findings are, they lack the force of the quantitative data we have collected. Before turning to the lessons that can be drawn from analyzing the survey responses, let us first examine the logic of causal direction in this case.

The scenario of reverse causation may be seen to hypothesize, in effect, that the ties are instrumentally constructed by actors expecting to benefit from them, or at least expecting that their political agenda will somehow be advanced through them. This assumed instrumentality of the ties, if we accept it as valid, serves as a mechanism inverting the direction of causality from what has previously been argued in this book. Such a suggestion that the ties represent an instrumental strategy of one subset of the leaders—namely, those already inclined to articulate their views through globalizing discursive horizons—fits easily within the assumptions of an enormously prominent social science perspective, the view that sociopolitical endeavors, and perhaps even social structure itself, are always best understood as the result of instrumental calculations and strategies. Thus it is appropriate to address the somewhat abstract possibility of reverse causation by examining the more tangible hypothesis of the ties' instrumentality.

One additional logical step is necessary before proceeding: if the ties do, in fact, represent a strategy intended to generate meaningful advantage of some sort, then clearly the ties should be perceived as useful by those who maintain them. Assessments of the ties' usefulness can, in this sense, stand as a marker of their instrumentality, although in some instances that marker may actually overstate the case for instrumentality. Where the perceived utility of the ties is high, that view could rest on (1) a *prior* assumption by those who do indeed instrumentally construct the ties in the expectation they will be useful, (2) an experiential judgment formulated *after* the ties have been built (for reasons apart from their presumed tangible benefits), or (3) some combination of (1) and (2). Thus any finding that the ties are judged to be useful should be seen as a necessary but not fully sufficient basis for the claim that they represent instrumental strategies.

Fortunately, the data include responses to a questionnaire item that directly takes up this theme. In the survey, we assessed the perceived utility of the ties as judged by the interviewed leaders. This simple and straightforward question allows us to address some rather complex issues. Let us now revisit the findings generated by this question which we briefly reviewed in chapter 2 (fig. 2.5, which is reproduced here as fig. 5.9).

As the data reproduced in figure 5.9 show, the relationship between the existence of the ties and their perceived utility is clearly identifiable, yet from the standpoint of an instrumentalist-only conception of social ties, the relationship is surprisingly weak. One-quarter of the leaders who maintain multiple ties, 25%, perceived those linkages as *not* useful. A somewhat larger proportion of the leaders with no ties, 40.9%, shared the view that worker–intellectual ties were not useful. If we focus instead on the most positive assessment of the ties' utility, that they are useful for both general and practical concerns, we find an even weaker relationship. The most positive view of the ties' utility is indeed slightly more prevalent among leaders maintaining ties: of those with multiple ties, 29.4% hold this most positive perception of the ties, whereas among the leaders lacking any connections to intellectuals the figure is somewhat lower, 23.9%.

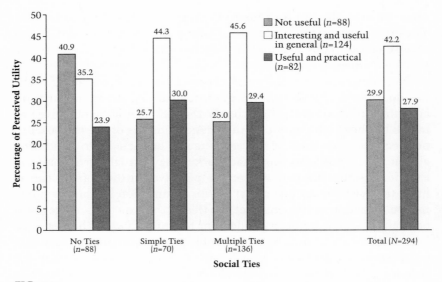

FIG. 5.9
Perceived utility by ties to intellectuals. The linear-by-linear test of association,
appropriate in this instance because of the symmetrical indicators, reaches
statistical significance at $p = .05$. However, the ordinal-by-ordinal test reaches
only marginal significance at $p = .06$.

Thus it is reasonably certain that leaders tied to intellectuals are a
bit more likely than their counterparts without such ties to see the
linkages as useful, but *the relationship between the two variables is
a relatively weak one characterized by numerous exceptions to the
most common pattern.* Many leaders maintain ties without believing them to be of any particular use, and many others without ties
nonetheless believe the ties to be useful. These quantitative findings
carry a very important substantive message: clearly, *the ties emerge
and survive—or fail to do so—for numerous reasons apart from the
belief that they will be useful.* Thus the ties cannot be taken as
an ironclad indicator of a prior instrumental desire to build such
contacts as a strategy intended to produce results.

This empirical finding reinforces a fundamental operating assumption of my research: social ties deserve to be examined as a potentially powerful independent variable—or causal factor—and not
simply as the presumed result of actor strategies. A long research tradition in sociology shares in this assumption. Indeed the pathbreak-

ing work of Mark Granovetter in *Getting a Job* argues explicitly that social ties that facilitate the search for employment are often not intentionally constructed in pursuit of that benefit but instead represent the by-product of other dimensions of social life unrelated to job search concerns.[10] This is not to argue that strategies and instrumental action are irrelevant in the construction of social ties. Clearly, in some instances, social ties do represent "investments" of entrepreneurial individuals who build them in the hope of attaining given benefits. However, social ties may emerge or disappear for numerous and disparate reasons, including routine childhood experiences, the geographic proximity rooted in residential patterns, joint schooling, mobility of all sorts, the indirect effects of one's friends' (or family members') sociability with others, and so on. *The many twists and turns in a person's biography constantly create and diminish—or even destroy—social ties for reasons often unconnected to any instrumental calculation of advantage.* And in a somewhat different (although related) vein, social structures of numerous sorts, including informal networks, help to shape individuals' social ties in ways those individuals may neither desire nor even be aware of. Finally, and most obviously, social ties of deep emotional content may be valued for their intrinsic worth irrespective of the external consequences they are likely to generate. Ties may or may not be instrumentally based.

Yet the issue we face here is not easily resolved in full. If ties can emerge either as the consequence of investmentlike instrumental behavior or as the unintended result of the routines, adventures, and flux in personal biographies, it remains to be determined whether the instrumentally based ties carry greater causal weight than the others. Only through multivariate analysis can we adequately assess this question. The issue is not easy to pose methodologically, for as I have emphasized, the judgment that the ties are useful may reflect either a strategic assessment predating the ties and at least partially responsible for their construction or an experiential impression formed only after the ties emerge for noninstrumental reasons. Thus the measure we have been examining, the perceived utility of the ties, may substantially overstate their instrumental underpinnings, but nevertheless this variable stands as our best opportunity to weigh the contribution of instrumental strategies to the seeming causal impact of the ties. Multivariate modeling of the data, to which we will now turn, shows strong confirmation of the view that the ties themselves, rather than any alleged prior strategy or design to construct them, carry the weight of causal explanation.

Assessing Competing Explanations through Multivariate Analysis

We have now reviewed evidence on the impact of a number of explanatory variables on democracy's public rhetorics but have yet to systematically assess their *relative* causal weight, a task we cannot reasonably avoid. There are two obvious reasons why it is important to do so: first, because variables we have found to be causally relevant in simple bivariate analysis may lose their explanatory power in multivariate work once we have controlled for the impact of other causal factors; and second, because systematic multivariate analysis offers a strong basis for drawing into one overall explanatory argument the various strands of causal analysis I have been developing. The simple cross-tabulations and bivariate analysis on which I have largely relied offer the great advantage of straightforward simplicity and the added benefit—unlike many advanced techniques of data analysis—of reporting full information on the distribution of *all* the cases. Despite these virtues, cross-tabulation is thoroughly unwieldy as a method for judging the relative causal weight of a substantial number of explanatory variables, and thus we shall now examine logistic regression models of the survey data. In these models we will be explaining the local leaders' predisposition to articulate globalizing discursive horizons; thus the dependent variable is a dichotomy, and logistic regression proves most appropriate.

The analysis reported in table 5.1 incorporates all those independent variables that, in the discussion thus far, have established a plausible claim to our sustained interest. Beyond that initial core, I add to the analysis five straightforward and potentially important variables not yet discussed: age in years, party membership, and three dichotomous variables that taken together report on the institutional position of the respondents in party leadership, union leadership, or some other institutional realm such as neighborhood associations, cultural endeavors, or social movements. Only two of these three dichotomous variables on institutional position can be included in any one model, and thus I report two models in order to assess the causal impact of all three institutional locations.

TABLE 5.1
Explaining globalizing discursive horizons through logistic regression (logistic regression coefficients, with standard errors in parentheses)

Independent Variables	Model 1	Model 2
Strength of social ties	.32*	.31*
	(.17)	(.17)
Opposition	.58**	.62**
	(.28)	(.28)
College education	.02	.02
	(.31)	(.31)
Age (in years)	−.02	−.02
	(.02)	(.02)
Theorists present	.32	.34
	(.32)	(.33)
Utility of ties	−.12	−.14
	(.18)	(.18)
Local autonomy	.22	.24
	(.27)	(.27)
Useful organizations	.11	.09
	(.11)	(.12)
Local efforts	.11	.10
	(.20)	(.20)
Party membership	−.80**	−.72*
	(.40)	(.40)
Institutional position		
Union	−.85*	.08
	(.49)	(.30)
Party	−.92*	N/a
	(.49)	
Other	N/a	1.46**
		(.60)
Constant	.40	−.44
	(1.06)	(1.05)
N	273	273
Model χ^2	26.22	29.19

Note: N/a, not applicable.
*$p < .10$ **$p < .05$ ***$p < .01$

The broadly inclusive models that result consist of twelve independent variables in each case, or thirteen all told including both models. I report the models first for the entire sample and then, in table 5.2, for both the postcommunist and socialist subcultures taken separately.[11] Six of the independent variables examined demonstrate a clear ability to help predict globalizing discursive horizons in at

TABLE 5.2

Explaining globalizing discursive horizons through logistic regression for each subculture (logistic regression coefficients, with standard errors in parentheses)

Independent Variables	Postcommunist		Socialist	
	Model 1	Model 2	Model 1	Model 2
Strength of social ties	.70***	.69***	−.07	−.12
	(.26)	(.26)	(.28)	(.27)
Opposition	.14	.17	.98**	1.07**
	(.43)	(.44)	(.42)	(.43)
College education	.32	.27	.44	.35
	(.47)	(.48)	(.53)	(.52)
Age (in years)	−.01	−.02	−.02	−.02
	(.03)	(.03)	(.03)	(.03)
Theorists present	.60	.60	−.05	.03
	(.49)	(.49)	(.53)	(.53)
Utility of ties	−.16	−.20	.14	.12
	(.27)	(.27)	(.33)	(.33)
Local autonomy	.63	.63	.21	.15
	(.41)	(.41)	(.44)	(.43)
Useful organizations	.13	.08	.17	.15
	(.19)	(.20)	(.18)	(.18)
Local efforts	−.22	−.21	.36	.32
	(.36)	(.36)	(.34)	(.34)
Party membership	−.54	−.43	−1.68**	−1.55*
	(.61)	(.62)	(.85)	(.85)
Institutional position				
Union	−.07	.47	−2.12**	−.26
	(.82)	(.46)	(.93)	(.48)
Party	−.52	N/a	−1.93**	N/a
	(.80)		(.96)	
Other	N/a	1.14	N/a	2.38**
		(1.02)		(1.18)
Constant	−.20	−.58	1.04	−.70
	(1.86)	(1.73)	(1.80)	(1.72)
N	135	135	118	118
Model χ^2	22.65	23.54	19.56	20.29

Note: N/a, not applicable.
*$p < .10$ **$p < .05$ ***$p < .01$

least one of the two subcultures, and/or the sample as a whole; the remaining seven variables show no such ability. The strength of ties proves extremely significant in the postcommunist subculture, whereas experience in the anti-Franco labor opposition proves highly significant in the socialist subculture. Both of these independent variables also prove useful in the analysis of the sample taken as a whole, but their explanatory impact is lower, and the level of statistical significance they attain is far weaker for the sample taken as a whole, especially in the case of the variable of most interest to us, strength of ties. Party membership and the institutional position variables prove highly useful for explanatory purposes in the socialist subculture, more weakly significant in the sample taken as a whole and essentially irrelevant in the postcommunist subculture. Perhaps what is most striking in these findings is that the causal processes at work in shaping discursive horizons are remarkably different in the two subcultures. The most important causal underpinnings of globalizing discursive horizons in each of the two subcultures are largely irrelevant in the other. For this reason it is more difficult to explain variation in the sample as a whole than in either of the two subcultures taken on its own, a theme to which we shall return in the next chapter.

These broadly inclusive multivariate models allow us to identify, on the basis of solid empirical evidence, six variables that offer substantial promise of explaining variations in democracy's public rhetorics. We will turn, in a moment, to an analysis limited to these most promising variables. By the same token, we can at this point exclude from our continuing analysis seven variables, most of which we have previously discussed and all of which pose important theoretical issues. These inclusive models, with twelve independent variables each, cannot conclusively demonstrate the complete causal *irrelevance* of these seven variables, but the models do offer an important test of their causal impact by allowing us to ascertain whether any variable that seemed earlier to contribute to globalizing discursive horizons remains in force or fades away once we have controlled for additional variables. For the seven variables we shall drop, the multivariate analysis offers *insufficient evidence* of any explanatory contribution to merit retaining them. Let us quickly review the variables we will now exclude.

The presence of internal theorists in the labor movement appeared to contribute to globalizing discursive horizons when we examined the variable through simple bivariate analysis, but once we control for a number of other variables, the explanatory value of this factor is substantially diminished, and it fails to attain a reasonable level of statistical significance. The Gramscian view emphasizing the special importance of internal theorists receives no direct confirmation here. The perceived utility of the ties, a variable of major theoretical import, also generates weak results. We find no evidence here that perceived utility, and thus a prior instrumental strategy, can be held responsible for both the ties and the globalizing rhetorics. Moreover, the fact that the ties do generate significant effects when controlling for their perceived utility substantially strengthens this book's argument that ties hold considerable causal power to reshape public life independent of the strategies and objectives that may have contributed to (or proved irrelevant in) the ties' genesis. Thus we find strong support, at least in this instance, for emphasizing social relations themselves, rather than instrumental strategies, as a fundamental explanation for variations in democracy's discursive horizons. Nonetheless, this is not to say that all social relations should be conceived to form one large aggregate category. The presence at the local level of organizations perceived by the respondents to be useful shows no significant explanatory effect in the inclusive multivariate model. Useful organizations proved earlier to be the strongest variable among those that could be placed within the "social capital" school, and yet this variable proves substantially weaker in multivariate analysis than the worker–intellectual social ties I emphasize. Local efforts, another measure that can be understood to capture a phenomenon of special interest to "social capital" theorists, namely, the predisposition of communities to engage in collective endeavors, also produces insignificant results in the logistic regression models.

One social background variable that had earlier seemed to hold some promise, and that some analysts might think more fundamental to political rhetorics than the social ties I emphasize, fails to generate convincing results in this multivariate analysis: despite the substantial bivariate relationship of college education to globalizing discursive horizons, once we have controlled for other variables, the effect diminishes substantially and fails to attain a level of statistical significance sufficient for retaining the variable. Moreover, the inclusion of college education as an independent variable clearly fails to erase the explanatory impact of social ties and other similarly useful variables. College education does increase the likelihood that leaders will maintain ties to intellectuals, but it is those ties, rather than education itself, that prove predictably useful in multivariate analysis. Local autonomy, a measure of the respondents' inclination to rely on locally based perspectives and experiences—as opposed to cues or political orientations emanating from national organizations—also fails to generate meaningful results. We thus find no evidence that globalizing discourse is meaningfully facilitated or

TABLE 5.3
Explaining globalizing discursive horizons through logistic
regression (parsimonious models) (logistic regression
coefficients, with standard errors in parentheses)

Independent Variables	Model 1	Model 2
Strength of social ties	.37**	.35**
	(.15)	(.15)
Opposition	.70***	.73***
	(.27)	(.28)
Party membership	−.73**	−.66*
	(.35)	(.35)
Institutional position		
Union	−.73#	.14
	(.46)	(.28)
Party	−.85*	N/a
	(.47)	
Other	N/a	1.43***
		(.59)
Constant	.08	−.84*
	(.49)	(.45)
N	285	273
Model χ^2	23.67	26.95

Note: N/a, not applicable.
#$p < .15$ *$p < .10$ **$p < .05$ ***$p < .01$

impeded by the strength of national organizations and their institutional discipline within local communities. Local autonomy, in formulating political initiatives, does not render more likely the narrow politics of defensive localism. Concrete, and frequently locally based, experiences and social relations—rather than the strength or weakness of the disciplinary reach held by national organizations—explain the leaders' predisposition to articulate globalizing rhetorics. Finally, one straightforward demographic variable I have yet to discuss, the respondents' age in years, fails to produce persuasive results. I report this nonfinding in order to eliminate any doubt that readers might hold concerning the possible explanatory contribution of age.

We focus next on a more parsimonious pair of models limited to the six independent variables (five in each of the two models) that have demonstrated a substantial explanatory contribution in the first pair of (comprehensive) models. As the data reported in table 5.3 show, in the sample taken as a whole, both the strength of ties and experience in the anti-Franco opposition contribute substantially to predicting globalizing discursive horizons; both variables generate

TABLE 5.4
Explaining globalizing discursive horizons through logistic regression by subculture (parsimonious models) (logistic regression coefficients, with standard errors in parentheses)

Independent Variables	Postcommunist		Socialist	
	Model 1	Model 2	Model 1	Model 2
Strength of social ties	.75***	.73***	.04	−.01
	(.22)	(.22)	(.26)	(.26)
Opposition	.30	.31	1.06***	1.13***
	(.41)	(.41)	(.41)	(.42)
Party membership	−.56	−.48	−1.45*	−1.37*
	(.54)	(.54)	(.77)	(.78)
Institutional position				
Union	−.18	.47	−1.52*	−.28
	(.72)	(.41)	(.81)	(.44)
Party	−.62	N/a	−1.24#	N/a
	(.73)		(.82)	
Other	N/a	1.18	N/a	2.25**
		(.96)		(1.17)
Constant	−.62	−1.30**	1.52#	.22
	(.77)	(.65)	(1.04)	(.85)
N	142	142	120	120
Model χ²	15.91	16.84	16.14	18.68

Note: N/a, not applicable.
#$p < .15$ *$p < .10$ **$p < .05$ ***$p < .01$

stronger findings here than in the comprehensive models, and the explanatory strength of participation in the anti-Franco movement appears especially strong. Party membership, and the institutional position of some leaders in activities other than union or party work—typically involving neighborhood associations or social movements—also make important contributions to explaining the leaders' predisposition to articulate globalizing discourses.

Nonetheless, these findings mask an enormous difference in the causal processes at work within the two subcultures. As the data in table 5.4 show, social ties very strongly shape discursive horizons in the postcommunist subculture, whereas historic involvements in the anti-Franco opposition (and to a lesser extent variables dealing with party membership and institutional position) exert a very large impact in the socialist subculture. Neither of these two variables, social ties and oppositional involvement, proves relevant in *both* subcultures. Thus we find that worker–intellectual ties may exert a very large impact on democracy's public rhetorics, but that impact, it is clear, is not universally present. It varies substantially by subculture. Likewise, the large contribution of oppositional experience to globalizing discursive horizons is also contingent on subcultural context. Paradoxically, the effect of oppositional experience makes itself felt in the subculture in which that experience was least prevalent (although not uncommon). In the communist subculture, where oppositional activity was the norm during the Franco period, this variable exerts no discernable effect. We will examine in the next chapter these and related questions relevant for assessing the generalizability or contextual specificity of my argument on ties and public rhetorics.

In the socialist subculture, the institutional position of leaders, and their membership in—or formal independence from—the Socialist Party, contributes to the likelihood that they will employ globalizing discourse. The most powerful of the institutional position variables, the dichotomous indicator of involvement in some form of activity other than union or party affairs, proves quite powerful. As the odds ratio for this variable shows, socialist subculture leaders whose primary institutional activity falls in the broad category of "other" endeavors are approximately nine times as likely to articulate globalizing discursive horizons as are their socialist subculture counterparts with more conventional institutional responsibilities in the union or party.[12] These individuals, who are strongly involved in social movements, neighborhood associations, or the like, are also tied in some way to the socialist union or party—the basis for them being placed in the socialist subculture in our analysis.[13] Yet that linkage to one or both of the main organizations of the subculture is balanced by their primary engagement in organizations or movements including a wide range of members, many of them distant from the subculture's institutional core. Conversely, party membership and the two most conventional institutional positions exert a *negative* impact on globalizing discourse in this subculture.

Let us review the fundamental difference we find in the causal underpinning of globalizing discourse in the two subcultures. In the postcommunist case, ties to intellectuals strongly increase the likelihood that leaders will globalize; indeed, those social ties more than double the prevalence of globalizing discourse, as the odds ratios indicate.[14] No other variable proves helpful in our effort to explain globalizing discourse in that subculture. In contrast, a very different picture emerges in the socialist subculture: ties to intellectuals prove irrelevant here, but the combination of conventional institutional involvement (in union and/or party) with a linkage to some movement-type activity—whether in the historic opposition to the Franco regime, or in some other movement or broad association in the contemporary period as captured by the variable denoting "other" institutional positions—is highly predictive of globalizing discourse. The two subcultures manifest very different causal processes.

These findings are important for our overall understanding of the social processes shaping democracy's public rhetorics: much of the creativity and energy required if political endeavors are to be framed in a discourse connecting the specific to the general, the local to the translocal, emerges from the local level itself—whether in the form of social ties or through actor-centered connections between conventional institutions and broader movements. Strong national institutions and prestigious (or infamous) national leaders may not, on their own, engender a form of democratic life capable of fully engaging the public. As Tocqueville suggested more than a century and a half ago, the vitality of democracy rests, in no small measure, on locally based social (and political) connections. One important qualification deserves mention: many of the crucial ties we find between intellectuals and workers initially emerged within the structure of parties or unions. Thus national organizations and institutions are highly relevant to the process we have examined but only insofar as social ties freely emerge within those structures or insofar as those involved in the conventional structures also participate in less institutionalized or more broadly based activities, and that cannot be taken for granted.

This analysis thus far yields two strong findings—the causal role of worker–intellectual ties and of oppositional or other movement experience—but as noted, both effects appear largely contingent on subcultural context. Thus we must ask whether these findings can be generalized beyond the contexts studied. It is to this issue that we now turn.

6 The Specific and the General for the Social Scientist

The Interpretive Reach of Our Analysis

A central preoccupation in the methodological writings of sociology's founding theorists—the relationship between specific empirical cases and broad conceptual concerns—highlights an unavoidable tension, or challenge, for empirically oriented social scientists. We aspire to understand outcomes and processes in the cases we actually study, and thus often focus, to one degree or another, on the specificities of those cases; we seek to address broad problems from the standpoint of generalizing concepts and theories, and thus often minimize the particularities we observe, preferring instead to emphasize general processes lacking any mark of the specific contexts we have studied. Yet this tension need not lead us to set aside either of our twin intellectual commitments: to know in some detail what is specific and to sketch in clear outlines what is general. In this book I have constantly tried to address broadly experienced problems, felt in numerous countries throughout the world, from the standpoint of data and stories gathered in forty-nine local contexts throughout Spain. Many of the claims I have made are highly specific in nature—for example, the discussion of the two subcultures within the Spanish Left—but this book's argument is quite broad in its assertions, attempting to link the existence of ties between socially dissimilar groups to the nature, and the intrinsic interest, of democracy's public rhetoric. I have endeavored to develop a line of argumentation with potential implications for countries throughout the world where social ties among those actively engaged in politics cross important group boundaries—or fail to do so.

Some readers may conclude that the emphasis found here on specifically Spanish explanations detracts from the broader cross-national objective, but I do not share that view. In facing this basic tension in social science research, I make the strong assumption—drawn from the long tradition of Weberian social science—that careful examination of case-specific phenomena actually *enhances* our ability to address general theoretical issues. Through rigorous scholarly analysis, we can build generalizing interpretations on the foundation of case-specific research. The most compelling analysis is one that can withstand the criticism of both case specialists and theoretically oriented generalists, one that examines specific and particular traits, using them as a vehicle to pose big issues. The specificities of a case cannot be swept under the rug, unless we are confident that no one will ever look there—and fortunately in the modern scholarly world there is always someone prepared to look under the rug in the hope of disconfirming or substantially modifying earlier analysis.

Without question, some elements of the phenomena discussed in this book are more or less specific to Spain. Enduring legacies of the Civil War (1936–39), the historical experience of the anti-Franco opposition, the form taken by the post-Franco transition to democracy, the political history of the various parties and unions, the economic and cultural makeup of the regions examined—these are but some of the points on which the explanations and analyses of this book have incorporated experiences or circumstances particular to Spain. In this respect, Spain is simply a country like all others: every society has its particularities, and those particularities are inevitably intertwined with the causal patterns social scientists can discern. Yet even though Spanish particularities are to be found in varying degrees throughout this book's story, there may well be much in the causal relations we have uncovered that applies outside and beyond the Spanish case. Perhaps most deserving of our attention, in the effort to sort out the relative weight of specific and more generalizable dimensions of the Spanish experience, is the contrast in the pattern taken by worker–intellectual ties within the two left-oriented subcultures.

On one level, that contrast is itself of general and theoretical interest, for it underscores the salience of *subculture* as a conditioning variable, even when the subcultures in question are not tightly knit and binding communities. But on another level this contrast offers us the ground on which to build a general argument about the conditions under which ties can remake rhetorics, and about the substantially dissimilar social processes that can underpin globalizing discourse, as I attempt in this chapter. This chapter offers a generalizing theoretical argument based on salient characteristics of the two subcultures examined in the research.

The Disparity between Socialist and Postcommunist Subcultures: Which Is the Exception?

Our findings offer us a clear and tangible way to assess whether the impact of social ties on discursive horizons is a phenomenon largely specific to Spain or one likely to be found in many other national contexts as well. Even in Spain the phenomenon is not a universal one, as my research strongly underscores. Intellectual–worker ties exert a powerful impact on discursive horizons in the postcommunist subculture but, at least on the face of it, manifest no causal importance in the socialist subculture. The question we must confront is, Which of these subcultures represents the "exception" and which represents a "rule," that is, which subculture represents a reasonably common pattern we might expect to find also outside Spain? If the strong impact of ties within the postcommunist subculture is substantially more "exceptional" than the socialist pattern we find in the data, then perhaps the causal argument presented in this book stands as an isolated exception to the pattern one would encounter in most contexts. My argument would then be compelling only if taken as a case study of the postcommunist subculture. Of course, it may instead be the socialist context that is the more "exceptional" of the two subcultures. In this alternative scenario, my argument may carry significant implications for many contexts and actors far removed from Spain and thoroughly ideologically distinct from the Spanish postcommunists. This framing of the question is, nonetheless, deceptively simple: it is likely that *both* causal patterns can be found in *some* settings outside Spain. There is no reason to assume that social ties outside Spain should always manifest the causal pattern found in one or the other of Spain's two left-oriented subcultures. But it is not sufficient to simply affirm that both patterns may be found in other national settings. The data afford us opportunities to address the question posed above and to specify *when* social ties are likely to reshape rhetorics.

One useful way to address this problem is by analyzing in some detail the impact of actual party membership on discursive horizons in the two subcultures, a relationship that proved significant in the multivariate analysis of the last chapter. It is worth reemphasizing here that I have placed respondents within the subcultures on the basis of party *and/or* union involvements. Thus actual party membership cannot be taken for granted in either subculture. Among both

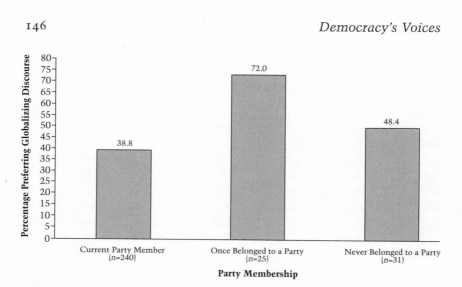

FIG. 6.1
Globalizing discursive horizons by party membership. When dummy variables are used for both "current party member" and "once belonged to a party" and the relationships are tested separately, only the relationship between party membership and adopting a globalizing discourse reaches significance at $p = .05$ or better.

the socialist- and postcommunist-oriented local leaders we interviewed, a substantial majority were members of a party—typically, but not always, the subculture's dominant party.[1] The remainder of the respondents, currently not belonging to a party, included some former members of a political party and others who had never belonged to a party. By distinguishing between these three groups—current members, former members, and lifelong nonmembers—we can see whether processes at work within each of the two dominant parties tended to inhibit or enhance globalizing discursive horizons among local leaders. As the data in figure 6.1 demonstrate, global discursive horizons are especially prevalent among *former* party members. Indeed, the drawing of connections between the specific and the general, the local and the extralocal, is nearly twice as common among former party members as among current members. These ex-members, most of whom currently hold leadership responsibilities within the union movement, include those who have given up their prior affiliation with one of the two major left-oriented parties and others who were once active in smaller minor parties. Finally, lifelong nonmembers fall in between the other two groups in their inclination to articulate political concerns through globalizing discursive horizons.

As the significance levels reported here show, we can be quite confident that current party membership is negatively associated with the tendency to articulate globalizing discursive horizons. Nonmembers are significantly more likely to employ globalizing rhetorics. Given the limitations on the sample size imposed by the intrinsically small numbers involved in our universe of study, there are relatively few cases of former members and lifelong nonmembers, thus making it difficult to achieve statistically significant findings for those categories, a difficulty reflected in the failure of these two groups to generate an acceptable level of certainty in the reported findings. Thus we should take the general finding on the difference between members and nonmembers as conclusive, whereas the results of the additional distinction between the two subcategories of nonmembers—and thus the finding on the special predisposition of former members to globalize—must be thought of as suggestive rather than conclusive.

It is only fair to note that if we choose to focus on absolute numbers rather than the relative percentages reported in the tables, we find that most local leaders who employ globalizing discursive horizons *are* currently party members. The fact that well over two-thirds of the sample is made up of current party members explains why the greatest number of globalizing leaders is to be found among current party members, even though in percentage terms such discourse is far more prevalent among former members and nonmembers. Nonetheless the impact of party membership on rhetoric is clear: current party membership seems to diminish globalizing discursive horizons in both subcultures, and the effect is especially salient (and statistically significant) within the socialist sphere, in which only 38.4% of party members are predisposed toward globalizing rhetoric (see fig. 6.2). This restraining influence on global discursive horizons is most definitely not an all-inclusive feature of the socialist subculture taken as a whole. As the data in figure 6.2 show, former party members in this subculture appear extremely likely to embrace globalizing discursive horizons. The absolute number of former members within the socialist subculture is quite small, making the precise finding reported substantially less meaningful than other percentages we examine, but notwithstanding this reservation it remains highly impressive that fully 100% of the

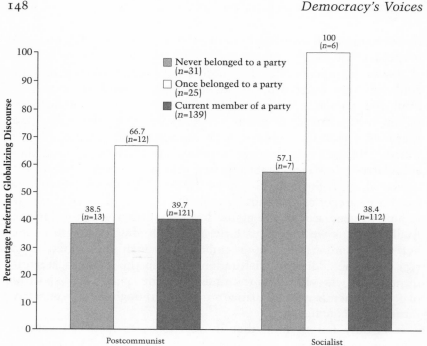

FIG. 6.2
Globalizing discursive horizons by party membership for each subculture. Relationships between "never belonged" and "once belonged" near significance at $p = .16$ in the postcommunist subculture and $p = .12$ in the socialist; party membership is significantly related to a globalizing discourse for socialists ($p = .05$).

respondents in this category prefer globalizing discourses. Lifelong nonmembers in the socialist subculture also manifest a rather favorable predisposition toward globalizing discursive horizons, as the data show. Thus current party members appear remarkably different from other participants in the socialist subculture.

The distribution of discursive styles among local leaders in the postcommunist subculture is noticeably different from that found among their socialist counterparts, as the data in figure 6.2 show. In the postcommunist subculture, globalizing discourse is roughly equally favored by party members and lifelong nonmembers; the difference between these two groups is just 1.2%, and the relationship is the inverse of what we found in the socialist subculture: in the more left-oriented subculture, party members appear very slightly more predisposed toward globalizing rhetoric than do lifelong non-members. One pattern, however, is similar to that found within the socialist subculture: former party members are those most likely to favor globalizing discourse in both subcultural contexts. Our initial examination of the data on party membership and discursive horizons in the subcultures thus yields two clear findings: current party members in the socialist subculture are relatively disinclined to embrace globalizing discourses, whereas former party members in both subcultures seem especially inclined to articulate such discourses. This pattern clearly suggests that it may be the Socialist Party, rather than the socialist subculture in general, that exerts a dampening influence on the ability of social ties to generate globalizing discourses. Later in this chapter, we examine what it is within the Socialist Party that holds primary responsibility for this pattern. It is essential to add that this restraining influence of the Socialist Party affects most strongly the causal power of social ties rather than the overall level of globalizing discourse, a puzzle to which we shall return.

The relatively small number of those respondents who were former members or lifelong nonmembers makes it difficult to generalize about these two categories, but one question is too important to be ignored—even if the numbers involved are insufficient for drawing a rigorous conclusion of the sort often permitted by large N survey analysis. Who are these former members within the socialist subculture? Or, to pose the question in slightly different terms, to which party or parties did the former members previously belong? If the former members had once belonged to the small far-left parties that largely disappeared after the years of transition to democracy, one could attribute these individuals' preference for globalizing discursive horizons to the enduring legacy of their previous involvement in a fringe of the communist subculture. Were this the case, the former members would, in a sense, represent the imprint of yesteryear's communist subculture within the contemporary socialist subculture. We might then be able to conclude that the roots of enthusiasm for globalizing rhetoric typically lay within the communist subculture. The empirical evidence, however, does not support such an interpretation: only six of the local leaders interviewed within the socialist subculture were former party members, but nearly all of these—five out of the six—were previously affiliated with the Socialist Party itself. The remaining individual, much like

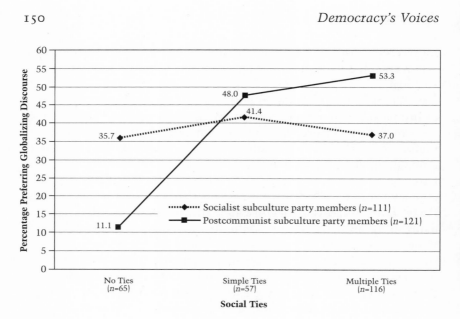

FIG. 6.3
Globalizing discursive horizons by strength of ties, for party members in two subcultures. Tests of statistical significance reveal that the relationship between the preference for a globalizing discourse and social ties for party members is highly significant for the postcommunist subculture ($p = .000$) but not for the socialist one.

several nationally prominent leaders within the Socialist Party, was a former member of the Communist Party. The unanimous embrace of global discursive horizons by these six former party members rests in all but one of the individual cases on a personal history of involvement within the Socialist Party itself. These findings underscore the need to examine more carefully the contrast between current party members themselves in the two subcultures.

The prevalence of party membership within the local leadership stratum of the two subcultures—and as a result, the relatively large number of respondents who fall within this category—makes it possible to compare the impact of social ties on discourse for party members in the different subcultures. As the data in figure 6.3 show, the impact of social ties among current party members is remarkably dissimilar in the two subcultures. In the postcommunist sphere, party-affiliated leaders with simple ties to intellectuals are far more likely (48%) than their counterparts without such ties (11.1%) to prefer globalizing rhetoric. The greatest predisposition toward such discourse (53.3%) is found among the leaders with multiple ties to intellectuals. Thus multiple ties generate an embrace of globalizing discourse nearly five times greater than that found among leaders lacking any ties to intellectuals, and local leaders with simple ties evidence nearly as great a tendency to globalize as do the leaders with more numerous ties. In contrast, the impact of ties is minimal among party members in the socialist subculture. Global discursive horizons are indeed slightly more prevalent among party members with ties than among those without ties, but in our data the effect is extremely weak and it is nonlinear. The highest predisposition toward globalizing rhetoric, 41.4%, is found among the socialist leaders with simple ties; an intermediate-level predisposition toward this discourse of connections, 37.0%, is present among the party members with multiple ties; and the lowest level, 35.7%, is evidenced among those with no ties to intellectuals. Although ties seem to increase ever so slightly the embrace of globalizing rhetoric, unlike the dynamic found in the postcommunist subculture, in this case more ties do not intensify the effect; a single tie generates a greater impact than do multiple ties. The weakness of these findings in the socialist subculture leaves us without any confidence that ties actually promote globalizing discursive horizons among Socialist Party members.

Alternative Lines of Interpretation

These findings suggest at least two alternative and substantially different lines of interpretation. Perhaps, we might hypothesize, the distinctive *ideological* orientation and historical legacies of the communist subculture generate especially meaningful ties between intellectuals and workers, ties with an unusually pronounced ability to redefine discourses. If so, then the causal dynamics highlighted in this book virtually require facilitating conditions largely specific to the postcommunist subculture. In this vein, one could easily argue that postcommunists (and communists before them) place greater emphasis than socialists on worker–intellectual linkages, on the basis of ideas central to their theoretical tradition as exemplified by the writings of Antonio Gramsci and even Lenin himself. Alternatively, one could argue that distinctive features of the socialist subculture—

at least during the period covered by my fieldwork in Spain—tended to diminish substantially the causal impact of worker–intellectual ties on public rhetoric. If this second line of analysis proves persuasive, one could then conclude that the ideological perspective and history of the postcommunist subculture are not in any sense essential for the ties to exert their causal impact. In this case it would still be necessary to search for the restraining influences within the Socialist Party that diminish the magnitude of the effect exerted by social ties.

One additional point of contrast merits attention: postcommunist subculture leaders without ties to intellectuals are substantially less likely to employ globalizing discursive horizons than are their counterparts—also lacking such ties—in the socialist subculture. Among leaders with ties to intellectuals, the postcommunist leaders are more inclined than their socialist equivalents to articulate a discourse of globalizing connections; among leaders without ties, the postcommunist leaders are much less so inclined. The ties command far greater causal power in the postcommunist sphere because of this dual pattern of difference.

We need not necessarily choose between socialist or communist "exceptionalism"; elements of both explanations reviewed here may help account for the striking difference in social ties' causal impact within the two left-oriented contexts. The ideological priority placed on intellectual–worker ties by many postcommunists may well contribute in some measure to the globalizing discursive horizons emphasized in this book, but the data strongly suggest that much of the explanation for the contrast between the subcultures must be placed elsewhere, namely, within the Socialist Party itself, rather than within the larger subculture to which it belongs. Both the survey data and qualitative findings clearly show that *socialist subculture leaders can manifest every bit as high a predisposition toward globalizing discourse as their postcommunist counterparts.* Thus the ideology and historical legacy of the communist movement are absolutely not necessary for local leaders to embrace globalizing discursive horizons.

The "voices" of socialist leaders—active in union and party—illustrate well the proclivity of many others within their subculture to articulate globalizing rhetorics. The Socialist mayor of a small industrial city in the Valencian region, speaking in city hall chambers carefully decorated with the abstract works of local artists, exemplified this generalizing spirit when he posed the question of whether Spain would "form part of the Europe of merchants or a social Europe." This globalizing approach took more practical direction when he explained his interest in addressing challenges of economic development from an extralocal perspective, noting that "if we are dealing with a world without borders we cannot limit ourselves to study our town [in isolation]."[2] At the other end of Spain, in a remarkably different industrial environment, a socialist unionist in the Nalón mining valley of Asturias spoke in even more emphatically globalizing terms. Before advocating an increased concern for Third World poverty, he noted, "The situation of the mining valleys cannot be good if the situation of Asturias is bad, and neither can the situation of Asturias be good if the national and international situation is unfavorable."[3] As these two cases suggest, many local socialist leaders globalize with eloquence and conviction. Socialists and postcommunists alike may be found defending local interests through proposals and rhetoric that reach well beyond their localities, and by the same token leaders within both subcultures can also often be found seeking to defend only very particular local interests. *What distinguishes the two subcultures from one another is the causal process* that helps determine if leaders will speak in the language of defensive localism or employ global discursive horizons. Quite concretely, *the contrast between the subcultures is rooted in a large disparity between current party members, a disparity centered not on the absolute predisposition toward globalizing discourses but instead on the strikingly dissimilar causal impact of ties to intellectuals (and other variables).* Such ties matter a great deal among postcommunist subculture party members and very little among socialist subculture party members. In contrast, former party members appear extremely inclined to embrace globalizing discursive horizons in both subcultures, and lifelong nonmembers are actually more so inclined in the socialist than in the postcommunist sphere. Apparently, ideology itself does not account for the differences observed; instead, social relations between intellectuals and local leaders in parties seem somehow substantially different in the two wings of the Spanish Left. If party membership status had proved largely irrelevant to our search for explanation, then we might attribute most socialist/postcommunist differences to the overarching ideological cast of mind and the associated traditions of the larger subcultures. The evidence, however, does not support such an interpretation.

Explaining the Pattern Found within the Socialist Party

The evidence raises a simple, obvious, and unavoidable question: Why do worker–intellectual social ties within the Socialist Party lack the causal force they exert within the other main political formation of the Spanish Left? One plausible hypothesis is that the sheer intensity of political debate and ideological passion is greater among the postcommunists, thus affording intellectuals—as the formulators and experienced communicators of ideas—with an especially important place in that subculture. The ties, as a consequence, would carry greater weight among the postcommunists than among their socialist counterparts. This hypothesis fits well with widely shared public images of Spain's left-oriented parties; at least two Spanish academics suggested this line of reasoning to me.[4] Nonetheless, the data offer a somewhat more complex explanation for the virtual causal irrelevance of worker–intellectual ties within the PSOE, even if there is some truth in that initial hypothesis emphasizing the greater intensity of ideological conviction in the postcommunist subculture.

Of the relevant findings already introduced, one fundamental if obvious point merits considerable emphasis: globalizing discursive horizons, as here defined, do not reflect a passion for abstract ideas and debate in isolation from practical and concrete proposals. Instead, these globalizing rhetorics constantly seek to establish connections between the specific and the general, the local and the extralocal, or the concrete and the abstract. It is the propensity to draw such connections that I identified in my field research as characteristic of working-class communities and leaders which globalize, whether because of social ties or other identifiable social configurations. Thus we need to explain why worker–intellectual ties, in contexts other than that of the Socialist Party, encourage local leaders to address practical problems in ways that generalize beyond the specifics of their locality. A passion for abstract ideas and ideology, where it exists, is not by itself sufficient to motivate and underpin the hard work involved in drawing *tangible* connections between concrete local problems and broader extralocal themes. The data we reviewed in chapter 2 suggest, in fact, that the two subcultures differ in the importance placed on actual practical matters in worker–intellectual interactions; postcommunist respondents were substantially more likely than their socialist counterparts to value ties to intellectuals as useful in practical terms. A willingness to take on practical problems is at least as important as a passion for abstract ideas in the configuration underpinning worker–intellectual ties in the postcommunist subculture.

It would clearly be grossly unfair and untenable to argue that Spanish Socialists lack a concern for practical politics and problem solving. Indeed, during their long tenure as the party of national government, from 1982 to 1996, the Socialists carried out numerous concrete policies of reform in areas such as health services, education, economic development, and public works.[5] Moreover, they have served as the party of local government for an even longer time in some municipalities and regions. As we shall see, it is precisely this experience in government, and its effect on the Socialist Party, that provides the best available explanation for the virtual causal irrelevance of worker–intellectual ties within the PSOE.

It is not my purpose in this book to review the numerous policy accomplishments (or disappointments) of the Socialists—or to assess the charges of the party's critics on themes such as corruption and the allegations of arrogance as well as the reversal of many traditionally left-wing commitments.[6] Indeed it would not be pertinent to the theme of this book to enter here the scholarly debate on the PSOE's governmental performance. Instead I examine the impact of national power on the Socialist Party itself, and thus by extension on the causal dynamics manifested by the social ties of its members.

Many of those I spoke with in the course of extensive qualitative interviews stressed the importance of political power in conditioning the role of intellectuals in that subculture. It should not be a surprise that an intellectual and political leader of the postcommunist subculture would make this point, arguing that national governmental power had influenced PSOE politicians, unionists, and intellectuals, significantly reducing their critical tendencies.[7] More striking is the fact that several figures within the socialist subculture itself made similar claims. A retired miner and socialist union activist in Asturias, himself a veteran of the socialist opposition to Franco, complained of the loss of critical tendencies among intellectuals and others in his subculture, asserting that "It is one of the diseases of power."[8] Somewhat more specific was an active socialist union leader in the Nalón mining valley who alleged that many intellectuals were drawn to the Socialists not by ideas or commitments but rather by power itself. As he formulated the matter, "There are many people who get on the winning bandwagon."[9] The view that many intellectuals were attracted by power, motivated more by their own interests than by broader commitments, was expressed by some intellectuals, including a socialist-oriented professor and political veteran in Asturias.[10] In a somewhat similar vein, prominent PSOE intellectual Ludolfo Paramio remarked to Paolo Di Rosa in a 1986 interview that intellectuals "have always pretended to speak on behalf of workers, when in truth they only intend to further their own interests."[11] Thus there is much evidence that power relations represented a major theme within the socialist subculture both for intellectuals and others. Existing research on the Socialist Party helps explain the organizational and political foundations of this emphasis on power.

Major political parties are typically diverse internally, and the Spanish Socialists are no exception. In one important respect, the party's membership base is relatively distinctive when compared to most other European social democratic parties: formal membership is extremely low as a percentage of party voters and sympathizers. Leonardo Morlino calculates formal membership in the PSOE as only 2.7% of the party's electorate in 1989, an extraordinarily low figure by European standards. Moreover, party membership was substantially lower before the Socialists won governmental power in the national elections of October 1982. As Morlino notes, "The most substantial period of membership growth by the PSOE occurred after, not before, its electoral triumph in 1982."[12] Thus party members, such as the local leaders interviewed, include individuals who joined the party during very different historical periods: under the difficult and repressive conditions of the Franco regime when the party was outlawed; during the fluid period of the transition to democracy and the early years of competitive politics before the party's electoral victory in 1982; and during the years of Socialist Party dominance in national politics. Party membership remained relatively low as a proportion of the socialist electorate and a substantial number of these members held some public office or position. The Socialist Party included numerous members with a long history of commitment to social reform through democratic politics, even at the risk of arrest and authoritarian repression during the Franco period.[13] Yet for many others, the party signified—in some instances to a degree overriding other considerations—an organization that could provide access to public positions and political power. The history of growth in party membership underscores this point. This is not the place to delineate or establish in depth the full range of local—and individual—variation in the meaning of Socialist Party membership and organization. In some (exceptional) local contexts, such as the mining valleys of Asturias, the socialist subculture represented a vital world built on the foundation of a genuine mass membership, a strong historical tradition, and collective leisure activities such as swimming pools administered by the local party. Nonetheless, the point requiring emphasis is that during the period of Socialist government in Madrid, for a significant number of party members, Socialist membership largely represented access to political power.

A certain concern for holding governmental power is of course a normal and healthy feature of political parties in democratic polities, but the magnitude of that concern—and more importantly, the space it leaves for the underlying or prior social commitments of a party—may vary from case to case. The survey data make it possible to assess how local leaders weigh the claims of state power against those of the labor movement activists. In a question I initially designed to measure attitudes toward the legitimacy of the state, I asked respondents to indicate if they considered it reasonable for the state to arrest and place on trial labor activists who had broken the law.[14] The question reads as follows:

> Many times in the labor movement—just as in other social sectors, such as the employers for example—actions which to some extent are illegal are considered and carried out. These actions can include unauthorized demonstrations, the non-observance of legislation on labor matters, encierros (shut-ins), etc., and may at times include holding a boss hostage. I would like to ask you about your opinions on what the state can do to respond to illegal actions of the labor movement. If the state arrests those involved and places them on trial, does this seem reasonable to you?

The respondents were offered the following six responses, each of which was read out loud to the interviewee and made available on a printed card listing all six options:

1. Yes it is reasonable because the state has the right and the duty to do so; if not the laws make no sense.
2. As long as we are talking about a democracy it is reasonable.

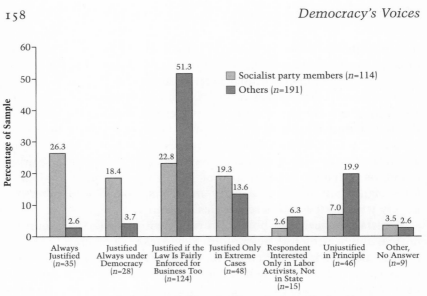

Attitudes toward State Legitimacy by Party Membership

FIG. 6.4
Attitudes toward state legitimacy when labor activists are arrested, by socialist party membership for Spain as a whole. Testing dummy variables for each possible response reveals statistical significance for all except "in extreme cases" and "interested only in labor."

3. In theory it is reasonable, but in reality many times the state enforces the law when it runs against our interests and does not enforce it when it runs against the interests of capital. So we have the right to insist that the law is enforced in a just manner.

4. It is reasonable only if we are talking about something very serious, such as holding a boss hostage, for example.

5. It may be that the state has the right to do so, but I am not interested in the rights of the state but rather in the interests of the workers.

6. It is not reasonable. What the state ought to do is respond to the needs and interests of workers and not arrest them.

The distribution of responses to this question among Socialist Party members is fundamentally different from that found among other respondents. As the data in figure 6.4 show, the single most common response among members of the PSOE is the first one. More than one-quarter of the Socialist Party members, 26.3%, affirm that it is always justified for the state to arrest and place on trial labor activists who have broken laws. Among the rest of the respondents, only 2.6% choose this response, making it the least common answer. Of course the attitudes expressed in the survey data clearly reflect the substantial diversity found within the Socialist Party. In contrast to the unqualified identification with state power of many PSOE respondents as mentioned earlier, a large proportion of them are reluctant to see the state use force against labor activists, although they accept the state's right, in principle, to do so—a somewhat ambivalent perspective expressed in both the third and fourth responses. A smaller proportion of the Socialist Party respondents expressed clear hostility toward the use of state power against labor movement activists who have broken the law, a point of view reflected in differing ways in the fifth and sixth responses. Still, the large number of Socialists who chose the first response is a striking finding that will likely surprise many readers familiar with Spanish history but perhaps less familiar with the nature of local Socialist organization in many Spanish towns. Law-oriented respondents who felt strongly that state authorities should be prepared to arrest law-breaking labor activists had available to them another clear and simple opportunity to express that view: the second response, which affirms that such state action is reasonable *as long as one is talking about a democracy.*

Authoritarian repression directed against democratic activists of all stripes, including labor movement members and many others as well, remained a recent and powerful memory when the fieldwork was carried out: our survey interviews were conducted less than fifteen years after the return of democratic freedoms for political and labor activists. In the early 1990s, numerous Spaniards then active— or once active—in politics had been arrested and tried for breaking laws, *but the large majority of such cases had taken place under Franco's regime of authoritarian repression, not under democracy.* By failing to insist that democracy and its freedoms are required if the use of state power against law-breaking activists is to be justified, leaders who choose the first response express an unconditional identification with state power so great that many proponents of democracy—be they on the right, left, or center—could find it troubling. Surely most interviewed leaders who choose the first response are proponents of democracy, but their failure to insist that democratic

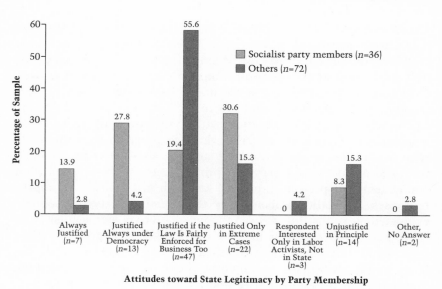

Attitudes toward State Legitimacy by Party Membership

FIG. 6.5
Attitudes toward state legitimacy when labor activists are arrested, by socialist party membership for Catalonia only.

freedoms are required for law enforcement to be legitimate suggests that their political sensibility is heavily weighed toward the identification with state power—rather than the defense of any values or principles with which such power might come into contact.

Substantially different are the Socialist Party respondents within the autonomous region of Catalonia.[15] In the Catalan context, where opposition to Franco's authoritarianism was extremely widespread and where the Socialist Party has a distinctive history and identity, many fewer local leaders identify uncritically with state power, as the data in figure 6.5 show. Indeed, if we focus on the overall distribution reflected in the survey, Catalan Socialists—by no means radical firebrands—are fundamentally unlike their fellow party members elsewhere in Spain in their pattern of response to this question. In a social democratic reform–oriented party such as the PSOE, one would expect to find party members searching for ways to effectively, and simultaneously, pursue various objectives, including reforms favorable to workers, the protection of the rule of law, and the consolidation of democracy. Clearly the Catalan Socialists manifested a more comprehensive concern for this overall set of objectives than did some of their party counterparts elsewhere in Spain, for whom the exercise of state power enjoyed unqualified support, thus taking precedence over other objectives.

These attitudinal data provide us with a promising avenue of interpretation to make sense of social ties' virtual causal irrelevance within the Socialist Party. For a rather large minority of party members—especially to be found among some of those who joined only after the party's massive electoral victory in 1982—power came to stand as an objective far more important than any of the principles or constituencies the party had traditionally sought to defend. Even for some within the majority in the PSOE who clearly maintained social democratic values, governmental power came to assume an importance so great that it largely eclipsed the independent significance of local communities and their demands.

Thus, for many in the Socialist Party, the government in Madrid consumed their energies and hopes—and more importantly, for our concern, stood as the great point of reference for their political interactions. Certainly the same could be said of many parties in power; one would be surprised if holding power had no effect on the sensibilities of a political party and its members. In a sense then, at the time of our interviews the PSOE stood as a case of a party in power, whereas the postcommunists were an opposition party that sought to mobilize people to pressure those in power for changes in policy. *This fundamental difference between parties in government and parties in opposition is probably at least as significant as ideology in shaping the causal power, or impotence, of social ties between workers and intellectuals.*

Moreover, parties in government are not all exactly the same in the extent to which holding power reshapes and dominates their political sensibilities. Our attitudinal data suggest, albeit through somewhat indirect evidence, that in the early 1990s the PSOE bore the imprint of holding power even more strongly than one might have assumed. The unqualified identification of many local socialist leaders with state power—manifested in the unconditional endorsement of arresting labor movement activists—reflects how deep that imprint was for many relevant actors in the party. Whereas many left-of-center parties maintain close, if sometimes strained, relations with previously sympathetic social movements even after they win governmental power, the Spanish Socialists suffered a complete collapse

of their relations with the union movement while they held governmental power.[16]

Ties-as-Conversation versus Ties-as-Brokerage:
A Concluding Argument

One other bit of evidence that we have already discussed can help
us draw out a broader causal argument on social ties' impact. Postcommunist subculture leaders are substantially more inclined than
their socialist counterparts to view the ties as actually useful in
practical terms. Apparently, for intellectuals and the local working-
class leaders connected to them in the postcommunist subculture,
interactions often afford a meaningful opportunity to discuss and
elaborate proposals, or strategies, that address local worker dissatis-
factions. Intellectuals may be involved in drafting (and helping to
conceive) position papers or proposals, economic analyses, or legal
appeals. In this sense the ties are of practical usefulness for many
local leaders. Thus, in the postcommunist context, ties are quite
likely to take the form of conversation, even if that conversation is
often an institutionally focused discussion of official union or party
projects rather than a less formal friendly chat. Worker–intellectual
connections in the postcommunist subculture are quite likely to take
the form of *ties-as-conversation*.

Why were the ties less likely to be seen as *useful* within the socialist context? We have no fully satisfactory survey evidence on this
point, but it seems likely that for many socialist intellectuals and
local leaders the crucial ties were those that connected them to power
holders in Madrid and not those that connected them to one
another—except insofar as their locally based ties did help to afford
access to power holders in Madrid. This interpretation builds on our
empirical findings—including qualitative fieldwork as well as the
direct survey evidence. We know that state power assumed great significance in the political sensibilities of socialist leaders at the community level and we know that these same leaders were disinclined
to see ties to intellectuals in the aggregate as practically useful.
In the socialist context it is reasonable to conclude that most
intellectual–worker ties did *not* involve conversations grappling with
the best way to focus local efforts on defending worker and community interests. Instead intellectuals and local working-class leaders

might interact at a party meeting, at a lecture reviewing general theories of social democracy, at a seminar on the European Union, at a dinner honoring a government minister. In these settings, the central government, the resources or solutions it might afford, and connections to that government were the most salient point of reference. Unlike worker–intellectual connections in the postcommunist subculture, which tend to focus on the effort to jointly formulate strategies and proposals for local mobilization to reverse social ills, the ties found in the socialist subculture typically did not generate *conversations* of the sort that could transform the discursive horizons of their participants. I argue that in the socialist subculture worker–intellectual connections (along with other ties within that subculture) typically took the form of *ties-as-brokerage* rather than ties-as-conversation. Although in ideological terms the postcommunist leaders were at least as strongly predisposed as their socialist counterparts to search for state-based solutions to social problems, the political location of the two cultures with respect to governmental power provided a fundamental difference in the meaning of worker–intellectual ties as experienced by local leaders. For the postcommunist subculture, social and political actors and individuals located outside the realm of central state power stood as the focal point of collective efforts and energies. Moreover, in the postcommunist case, there were very few resources of power to be allocated or pursued through brokerage.

Our findings show that in one Spanish context, ties have great causal significance for public rhetoric, whereas in the other they do not. The survey data and qualitative evidence lead us away from the easy hypothesis that ideological traditions can explain this pattern; instead, I have argued that the basis for this difference is to be found in the nature of the ties and in the relationship of the two subcultures to governmental power. *Ties-as-conversation, as typically found in the postcommunist subculture, transform rhetoric and encourage community leaders to articulate local problems through global discursive horizons. Ties-as-brokerage, as typically found among the socialist leaders, are much less likely to transform rhetoric.*

I understand brokerage to entail the actual dispensing of access to power and power-based resources or, at a minimum, the facilitation of instrumental exchange, which would likely not occur absent the broker's intermediation. Of course, brokerage is a phenomenon that plays important functions in sociopolitical life, as numerous analysts have emphasized.

The argument presented here should not be taken as a critique of brokerage. Moreover, in practice, conversation and brokerage may well overlap and coexist with one another. Nonetheless, there is a fundamental difference between social connections that center on the discussion of proposals, ideas, strategic analyses, and arguments—often valuing discussion itself as intrinsically worthy—and others that center more on the pursuit or exchange of power-based resources. The center of gravity in a system of social ties may fall rather strongly within one type of tie or the other: conversations versus brokerage.

A brief qualification is in order.[18] I do not in any sense intend the distinction between ties-as-conversations and ties-as-brokerage as a fully exhaustive conceptualization of all ties. Many social ties may not fit either of these two types, and furthermore, some ties may combine conversation with brokerage. The distinction is intended as a heuristic tool that helps clarify differences between the two subcultures studied here and that offers an approach likely to prove fruitful for extending this analysis to other settings.

This discussion suggests a paradox requiring our attention: most conventional analysts would likely assume that ties as brokerage are more practically useful than ties as conversation—exactly the reverse of what I argue here. Under close examination, this seeming paradox is readily resolved. The conversations I have identified as fundamental to the social processes shaping democracy's voices typically entail discussions about political strategies, projects, and plans; in that sense these conversations are useful for those concerned with political action and discourse. The ties-as-brokerage are surely practically useful in particular instances, but in a system of ties focused on access to power and its resources, many ties may *not* prove to be particularly useful. In a subculture heavily focused on power, broad categories of ties, such as the worker–intellectual connections on which I focus, may be perceived as generally lacking in practical usefulness, even if some particular ties within that broader category are thought to be highly useful. It is reasonable to assume that the ability to converse is substantially more widely diffused among the locally based actors we examine than is the direct access to national power and its resources. Thus most intellectual–worker encounters hold the *potential* to generate meaningful conversations insofar as those involved value such conversation, but most intellectual–worker ties are unlikely to offer their participants new access to power, newly "brokered" avenues to governmental resources, and influence. A subculture oriented toward power and brokerage is, for this reason, less likely to regard worker–intellectual ties as practically useful than is a subculture that values conversation as well as political mobilization and discourse. In any event, regardless of the judgment that we— or social actors themselves—draw about the relative usefulness of these two types of ties, our findings clearly show that ties-as-conversation, but not as brokerage, hold the ability to remake democracy's public rhetorics.

The fundamental contrast in the causal power of social ties between the two subcultures poses an obvious question: What *are* the social underpinnings of globalizing discourse in the socialist subculture—if indeed there are *any* that prove identifiable? After all, local socialist leaders appear, in the aggregate, every bit as predisposed toward articulating global discursive horizons as are their postcommunist counterparts. In fact, the findings examined in chapter 5 unmistakably show that there *is* an identifiable social configuration underpinning globalizing discourse in the socialist subculture. Among Spanish socialists, that causally relevant configuration rests on the juxtaposition of institutional political involvement—whether in union or party—with a history of participation in a broader movement, such as the anti-Franco opposition or some contemporary social movement. In this subculture, where institutional political life was heavily focused, at the time of my research efforts, on the exercise of national governmental power, ties located within the subcultures' primary institutions offered no guarantee of encouraging globalizing discourse, but the experience of many subculture leaders in movements located *outside* the realm of institutionalized politics did offer fertile ground for such rhetorics. To put the matter slightly differently, for Spanish socialists, the social processes generative of globalizing discursive horizons involve the juxtaposition of participation in *both* the subculture's institutionalized nucleus and broader movements more loosely associated with that institutional core. This dual experience serves as a rough functional equivalent to the postcommunist subculture's boundary-crossing social ties and the conversations they represent. The social underpinnings of globalizing discourse are identifiable in the two cases, but they differ. In the subculture within which ties take the form of conversation, the ties themselves carry the ability to reshape public rhetorics. In the other subculture, where ties-as-brokerage have been more common, the social underpinnings of globalizing discourse rest not on ties but on the movement–institutional core juxtaposition.

The clear implication of these findings is that where political (or social) forces external to state power attract the collective energies and hopes of those politically engaged, and where ties such as the linkages we examine between intellectuals and workers take the form of conversation, those ties can substantially transform public rhetoric. But where central state power occupies the attention and imagination of those politically engaged, ties are much more likely to take the form of brokerage, and thus are likely to have much less impact on discourse. Thus the pattern found in the postcommunist subculture should prove generalizable to many contexts outside Spain and many movements ideologically unlike the Spanish post-communists. But the socialist subcultural pattern is also certainly found outside Spain. These two patterns exemplify widely contrasting relationships between local political action and national political power—a theme of Tocquevillean vintage. The causal impact of social ties on democracy's public rhetoric can surely be found in many contexts outside Spain, but not in all contexts.

7 Beyond These Towns and Valleys

The Larger Significance of Democracy's Voices

This book's endeavor to identify social processes underpinning globalizing discursive horizons would stand as a hollow enterprise if I failed to make a compelling case that the argument *matters* for outcomes of broader concern. We need to establish that globalizing discursive horizons do matter—at a minimum for the quality of democracy's public life, if not for other reasons as well. Moreover, we need to explore the implications of arguing that social ties, rather than simply institutional design or the actions of prominent leaders, shape the quality of public life. Thus we must ask whether the causal argument on social ties carries any meaningful practical consequences. Finally, we need to seriously examine whether I have reached too far in arguing that boundary-crossing social ties can remake public life insofar as those ties take the form of conversation. After all, the data focus on one particular *variety* of such ties, namely, connections between intellectuals and workers. To what extent do this book's findings apply to other boundary-crossing social ties, apart from worker–intellectual contacts? In these concluding pages we will briefly review all these questions, although a fully adequate response requires work and analysis by others. It is ultimately only through an ongoing scholarly conversation that these difficult questions can be fully resolved.

Weighing the Significance of Discursive Horizons

At least two important scholarly perspectives in democratic theory offer a strong basis for the judgment that globalizing rhetorics enhance democracy's quality. Theoretical efforts to adapt democratic

thinking to major changes in the contemporary world stand alongside a major theoretical tradition emphasizing the potential that
democratic debate may hold for changing opinions through discussion—rather than simply recording set and unchanging viewpoints—
in offering us a firm intellectual grounding for the claim that
globalizing discourse serves democracy's quality.

Perhaps the most prominent theoretical claim on the need to adapt
democracy's horizons to meet the challenges posed by worldwide
change is the stimulating work of David Held. Held's analysis of
democracy in an age of globalization, as manifested in his advocacy
of "cosmopolitan democracy," emphasizes the importance of forging
"a transnational, common structure of political action." Given the
growing relevance of processes and problems transcending national
boundaries and preexisting political communities, Held sees great
value in the political efforts "seeking to create new forms of public
life and new ways of debating regional and global issues."[1] Thus one
of the most influential attempts to remake democratic theory for an
age of globalization provides us ample reason to find great value in
the ability of local political actors to articulate their concerns in
terms that are translocal and that illuminate connections, processes,
and solutions of global scope.

Perhaps even more relevant for evaluating the significance of globalizing discursive horizons is a major school in political theory, the
scholarship on "deliberative democracy." In his important contribution to the work on deliberative democracy, Jon Elster emphasizes
that politics based on discussion, argument, and (potentially) persua-
sion—rather than the mechanical counting of set preferences or
the bargaining for advantage among established interests—requires
political actors to formulate their agendas in ways that transcend, or
appear to transcend, the narrow defense of self-interest.[2] Thus if
democratic politics is to build spaces and opportunities for *deliberation*, fulfilling the aspirations of numerous prominent political
thinkers, it is essential for democracy's agendas to be articulated in
ways that build connections and that establish linkages between
locally experienced problems and translocal realities. It is difficult to
see how narrow defensive localism—or any form of transparently
self-interested politics—can contribute to genuine deliberation rather
than simple bargaining. Globalizing discourse, in contrast, seeks to
engage broad and geographically dispersed publics, whether in agreement or disagreement, and thus invites both debate and deliberation

over its broad analyses and proposals. The effort and skill required to articulate political agendas conducive to extralocal debate and deliberation are considerable; globalizing discursive horizons cannot be taken for granted, as my empirical analysis amply demonstrates. Thus the causal dynamics identified here contribute substantially to underpinning democracy's quality—unless we view theoretical claims on deliberative and cosmopolitan democracy as empty musings. If the political essence of democracy includes the forging of spaces and opportunities for deliberation, and if globalization in the economy stands as a challenge for democratic politics, then the broad discursive horizons emphasized here carry great significance for democracy's quality.

Recent work in cultural sociology offers a somewhat different yet complementary perspective on the significance of discursive horizons. As Mabel Berezin has noted, the broad terrain linking culture to politics stands as an area of major creative work focusing on many phenomena, including political discourse.[3] In his highly suggestive recent book, *Cultural Dilemmas of Progressive Politics*, Stephen Hart argues that social and political movements vary not only in the interests or ends they defend but also in the cultural work they undertake to craft and enliven their message, in the modes of discourse they employ in communicating.[4] Hart distinguishes between what he calls *constrained* and *expansive* discourses, a formulation similar but not identical to the contrast drawn here between discursive horizons that are defensive and localistic as opposed to those that globalize. For Hart, the primary issue is whether activists weave together specific concerns and large principles, whereas in my analysis the focus lies on the spatial points of reference articulated in political discourse. Yet these two ways of distinguishing between relatively narrow and rather broader discourse complement one another strongly.

If Hart is right in arguing that the progressive movements on which he focuses have been frequently handicapped by a relative deficit in their ability to constitute robustly expansive discourses, then my argument identifying social processes underpinning globalizing rhetorics takes on added significance. Indeed, for all those concerned with the ability of *any* movement to forge a broadly compelling case capable of reaching national (or international) publics, this book's search for causal processes that shape discursive horizons should prove meaningful. The identification of clear patterns of variation in political discourse, and its cultural content, stands as an important contribution of work such as that of Hart, but such contributions serve to further accentuate the need to locate underlying causal processes responsible for forging rhetorics. Globalizing discursive horizons and the conversations on which they are often based help to generate a style of politics that many analysts in more than one scholarly field find meaningful. The connection between the local and the extralocal here emphasized stands as an important theme not only in politics but also in a broader array of arenas, as underscored by the important ongoing work of Sidney Tarrow and others.[5]

The ability of globalizing discourse that has emerged in local communities to contribute to the broader public discussion—and thus to the quality of democracy—seems evident, but admittedly the patterns discussed here are not the only determinants of democracy's quality. A vibrant public sphere requires more than globalizing discourse. It requires a rather broadly shared interest in listening to and engaging such discourse. For some power holders (and citizens), many of democracy's voices are of little if any real interest. Macrolevel political variables, traditions, and processes may help account for national differences in elites' engagement—or denial—of democracy's divergent voices.[6] Having said this, defensive localism and globalizing rhetorics offer markedly different claims on the public attention; they are fundamentally dissimilar in their potential to engage a national audience, and set of players, in public discussion.

Practical Import of Social Ties

In this volume I have made a strong case that social ties often carry the power to remake public rhetorics, but I have not established that this claim holds any real meaning outside fairly specific disciplinary debates in the social sciences. Thus we must ask whether this explanatory emphasis on social ties carries any practical import. For many analysts of social ties within the network school, ties reflect *structures* of association, friendship, and linkage, both direct and indirect. Yet given this book's focus on two-way dyadic ties between workers and intellectuals, and in light of our discussion concerning the multiple origins of ties, there is no need to conceive of the linkages examined here as "structural" in nature. Ties emerge or fade away for many reasons often including effort, decisions, and patience.

The most direct practical implication of this book's causal argument is that in the aggregate, the numerous small efforts and decisions involved in making—or unmaking—social ties help to shape the democratic public arena. Ties that cross important group boundaries require effort and patience if they are to be sustained and, above all, if they are to include genuine *conversation*, listening as well as talking. Perhaps in part because of the effort such ties may require, contacts between intellectuals and workers have tended to decline, but the future trajectory of boundary-crossing ties cannot be fully known. Our findings show that the numerous small decisions involved in building or abandoning such ties, in listening patiently or avoiding conversation, stand as a meaningful form of human action with significant consequences for the character of public life. Public rhetorics that engage or disengage their listeners often rest on microlevel patterns of social connection and conversation on the part of the leaders articulating those rhetorics. This book's causal argument suggests that the ultimate responsibility for the flourishing or decay of democracy's public life is more widely shared than many might assume. Small questions that countless citizens confront concerning whom they associate with, listen to, and engage in conversation with, carry—in the aggregate—large consequences for democracy's public quality.

In this sense our findings clearly show that despite their enormous importance, institutions alone cannot guarantee the quality of democracy's public sphere of debate. Many of the ties we find to be important initially emerged within institutions, but many others did not. Thus this book's argument suggests that one contribution of institutions to democratic quality is indirect and incomplete: formal structures such as unions and parties may help to foster *some* causally crucial social ties, whereas other such ties may emerge *outside* the boundaries of formal institutions.

Are Intellectual–Worker Ties Distinctive?

I have presented a rather general argument about the causal power of boundary-crossing social ties, thus reaching somewhat beyond the actual empirical substance of our research findings on intellectual–worker connections. To what extent is this broad reach justified? After all, intellectual–worker ties are *distinctive* in some respects, as a long theoretical tradition has emphasized, and that distinctiveness might be thought at least partially responsible for the ability of the ties we have studied to reshape public discourse.[7] It is important to recognize that some specific features of intellectual–worker connections—as opposed to general features of boundary-crossing social ties—can be theorized to contribute to rhetorics of the sort understood here to represent globalizing discursive horizons. Indeed sociologist Dick Flacks has argued that intellectuals are especially well suited to encourage social movements to avoid particularistic claims and to develop generalizing discourses. Writing approximately a decade ago, he argued that "There is a need for some people to take responsibility for . . . teaching everyone else [in social movements] to see how their local experience is connected to the global."[8] Flacks's highly insightful claim that intellectuals could play just such a role appears to be strongly confirmed by my findings.

On close examination, however, it is not clear that the causal force of our findings can be confined exclusively to intellectual–worker ties, rather than boundary-crossing connections taken somewhat more broadly. The survey data clearly showed that intellectuals have not generated any given ideological perspective on the part of those tied to them. Moreover, the qualitative interviewing showed that the intellectuals making the greatest impact on workers were those who knew how to listen, who engaged in conversation. Thus our research suggests that at least in the case of causally relevant social ties, intellectuals have not engaged in an asymmetric process of "teaching" workers one or another theoretical perspective. Intellectuals do often theorize, but the most causally significant worker–intellectual linkages did not take the form of theoretical seminars or, worse still, lectures. The learning and theoretical leanings of many intellectuals may well play some role in the causal dynamics we have encountered but that role is likely far more limited than some scholars have assumed.

The broader claim emphasizing the importance of boundary-crossing social connections between political leaders and others socially unlike them also holds a strong place in prior scholarship. Especially relevant is the extraordinary contribution of Christopher Lasch, *The Revolt of the Elites and the Betrayal of Democracy*. Lasch argues that democratic debate and public life have entered into a serious state of decay in the United States largely because the elites—responsible for public life and political debate—are increasingly cut off from those socially dissimilar, especially in the working class. Lasch tellingly laments "the absence of institutions that promote general conversation across class lines [thus yielding a context in which] conversation has become almost as specialized as the production of knowledge."[9]

Despite the wealth of data that we have reviewed, it is not possible to fully resolve the question of whether the social processes underpinning globalizing discursive horizons are better captured by Lasch's broad concern over the declining social connections of elites—and the loss of cross-class venues for conversation—or by more specific theories focusing exclusively on workers and intellectuals. Surely, future work by scholars will contribute to answering this question. Yet the ultimate answer to this query lies not only in scholarship but also in the ties and conversations of countless citizens.

Even if intellectual–worker ties prove especially likely to engender globalizing discursive horizons, that in no way diminishes the potential significance of other cross-class connections insofar as they take the form of conversation. After all, a central finding of this study is that the ties that most influence public life are those in which the participants listen to one another. A local union leader in a small textile town with few ties to intellectuals put the matter very well when he related a remark he had recently made to union delegates gathered in a districtwide assembly: "We are all, in a way, teachers and students."[10] With these simple words, he called on the union delegates to listen, learn, and offer ideas in their conversations with workers they represented. Yet if this book's argument is well placed, conversations will prove especially valuable in reshaping rhetorics when they join together socially dissimilar persons whose perspectives and discourse can grow through the experience. Boundary-crossing ties and conversations not only inside official political institutions but also beyond their formal limits can help build a democratic public sphere in which the desire of high school students in the Nalón coal valley, as well as countless others, to "speak, express, write, narrate" leads to debate and discussion that citizens can follow with interest, rather than narrowly focused clamorings that would-be listeners seek to block out.[11] Democracy's quality rests in large measure on rather simple, yet increasingly uncommon, social foundations.

Notes

Chapter 1. The Quality of Democracy

1. See *El Periodico de Catalunya*, June 11, 1994, 68.

2. The extensive literatures on the conditions for democratic politics, transitions to democracy, and the consolidation of democratic rule provide a strong intellectual foundation for analyzing the quality of democratic life. Classic and more recent works that continue to be must reading for those working in the field include (in order of publication) Robert Dahl, *Polyarchy: Participation and Opposition* (New Haven: Yale University Press, 1971); Guillermo O'Donnell, Philippe Schmitter, and Laurence Whitehead, eds., *Transitions from Authoritarian Rule: Prospects for Democracy* (Baltimore: Johns Hopkins University Press, 1986); Adam Przeworski, *Democracy and the Market* (Cambridge: Cambridge University Press, 1991); Samuel Huntington, *The Third Wave: Democratization in the Late Twentieth Century* (Norman: University of Oklahoma Press, 1991); Scott Mainwaring, Guillermo O'Donnell, and Samuel Valenzuela, eds., *Issues in Democratic Consolidation* (Notre Dame, Ind.: University of Notre Dame Press, 1992); Juan Linz and Alfred Stepan, *Problems of Democratic Transition and Consolidation: Southern Europe, South America and Post-Communist Europe* (Baltimore: Johns Hopkins University Press, 1996). This is not the place for a full discussion of ongoing developments in this vast literature.

3. See Alex Hadenius, ed., *Democracy's Victory and Crisis* (Cambridge: Cambridge University Press, 1997). On the breakdown of democracies, see the now classic work of Juan Linz and Alfred Stepan, *The Breakdown of Democratic Regimes* (Baltimore: Johns Hopkins University Press, 1978). This volume holds much relevance for studies of transitions to and the consolidation of democratic regimes.

4. I distinguish between the *authenticity* of democracy—which is to say the extent to which a political system meets the minimum defining conditions for a modern democratic regime—and democracy's *quality*, which I understand to refer, in one way or another, to a political system's degree of success in fulfilling certain aspirations that arise within, or are associated with, democratic polities. On the minimum defining conditions for democracy, see Philippe Schmitter and Terry Lyn Karl, "What Democracy Is and Is Not," *Journal of Democracy* (summer 1991): 75–88. In this book's conclusion, I return to the theme of democracy's quality.

5. Robert Putnam, with Robert Leonardi and Raffaella Nanetti, *Making Democracy Work: Civic Traditions in Modern Italy* (Princeton: Princeton University Press, 1993).

6. Many theorists and analysts of democracy are currently grappling with the conceptualization of democracy's quality. For a recent discussion emphasizing conditions and requisites for the agency of citizens, see Guillermo O'Donnell, "Human Development/Human Rights/Democracy," paper prepared for the Workshop on the Quality of Democracy, United Nations Development Program, and Programa Estado de la Nación, Costa Rica, September 2001. For stimulating recent work on political talk, or its absence, in the American context, see Nina Eliasoph, *Avoiding Politics: How Americans Produce Apathy in Everyday Life* (Cambridge: Cambridge University Press, 1998). See also the earlier influential study by William Gamson, *Talking Politics* (Cambridge: Cambridge University Press, 1992). The literature on "deliberative democracy" is quite large. For an influential collection of essays on this perspective, see Jon Elster, ed., *Deliberative Democracy* (Cambridge: Cambridge University Press, 1998). On the heterogeneity of the tradition of political discourse, see Seyla Benhabib, "Models of Public Space: Hannah Arendt, the Liberal Tradition, and Jürgen Habermas," in *Habermas and the Public Sphere*, ed. Craig Calhoun, 73–98 (Cambridge: MIT Press, 1992).

7. Alexis de Tocqueville, *Democracy in America*, trans. George Lawrence and ed. J. P. Mayer (New York: Harper Perennial, 1969); John Stuart Mill, *Considerations on Representative Government* (New York: Liberal Arts Press, 1958); Hannah Arendt, *The Human Condition* (Chicago: University of Chicago Press, 1958); Craig Calhoun, ed., *Habermas and the Public Sphere* (Cambridge: MIT Press, 1992); Christopher Lasch, *The Revolt of the Elites and the Betrayal of Democracy* (New York: Norton, 1995). For an excellent discussion of the republican tradition in political thought, see Josep Lluís Martí Mármol, "El republicanismo: El renacimiento de una tradición filosófica-política," *Leviatán*, forthcoming.

8. Garry Wills, *Lincoln at Gettysburg: The Words That Remade America* (New York: Simon and Schuster, 1992) 20, 38.

9. For an overview of this and other core ideas in sociology, see David S. Hachen, *Sociology in Action* (Thousand Oaks, Calif.: Pine Forge, 2001).

10. The two great works of Tocqueville, which should be read in conjunction with one another, are *Democracy in America*, and *The Old Regime and the French Revolution*, trans. Stuart Gilbert (New York: Anchor Books, 1955).

11. Despite the debate between them, the intellectually rich recent contributions of both Theda Skocpol—and other contributing authors along with her co-editor Morris Fiorina—and Robert Putnam emphasize primarily the contributions of formal associational membership to civic life. See Theda Skocpol and Morris Fiorina, eds., *Civic Engagement in American Democracy* (Washington, D.C.: Brookings Institution Press; New York: Russell Sage Foundation, 1999); and Robert Putnam, *Bowling Alone* (New York: Touchstone Books, 2001). Sociologist Robert Wuthnow also stresses newer and looser forms of association in Wuthnow, *Loose Connections: Joining Together in America's Fragmented Communities* (Cambridge: Harvard University Press, 1998).

12. To be fair, some neo-Tocquevilleans do mention informal social relations—such as spending time with family or friends—albeit with substantially less emphasis than they place on formal organizational membership.

13. Peter Bearman, *Relations into Rhetorics: Local Elite Social Structure in Norfolk England, 1540–1640* (New Brunswick, N.J.: Rutgers University Press, 1993); Roger Gould, *Insurgent Identities: Class, Community, and Protest in Paris from 1848 to the Commune* (Chicago: University of Chicago Press, 1995).

14. Among the theorists who have written suggestively on this theme from widely divergent perspectives, several of the most important are Gramsci and Lenin; Raymond Aron, *The Opium of the Intellectuals* (Lanham, Md.: University Press of America, 1985); Joseph Schumpeter, *Capitalism, Socialism, and Democracy* (New York: Harper and Brothers, 1947); Selig Perlman, *A Theory of the Labor Movement* (1928; reprint, New York: A. M. Kelley, 1949); and Robert Michels, *Political Parties: A Sociological Study of the Oligarchic Tendencies of Modern Democracy* (New York: Free Press, 1962).

15. In fact, worker–intellectual linkages have played an important historic role even in the United States, as emphasized by a group of scholars and public intellectuals who recently called for their renewal. See Steven Fraser and Joshua Freeman, eds., *Audacious Democracy: Labor, Intellectuals, and the Social Reconstruction of America* (Boston: Houghton Mifflin, 1997). This volume originated in a public "teach-in" held at Columbia University in 1996.

16. In my survey interviewing for *Working-Class Organization and the Return to Democracy in Spain* (Ithaca: Cornell University Press, 1990), I encountered numerous workplace union leaders who actively maintained contacts with the intellectual world.

17. For an analysis of differences between public and hidden expressions of political sentiment or dissatisfaction, see James Scott, *Domination and the Arts of Resistance: Hidden Transcripts* (New Haven: Yale University Press, 1990).

18. For a complete scholarly edition of Gramsci's central writings, see Antonio Gramsci, *Prison Notebooks*, ed. with an introduction by Joseph Buttigieg (New York: Columbia University Press, 1992).

19. Tocqueville's analysis of his native France is most fully developed in *Old Regime and the French Revolution*. The comparison between France and the United States is constantly present in his thinking as reflected in his earlier and most influential work, *Democracy in America*.

20. In addition to those already cited, see the important contributions of Lewis Coser, *Men of Ideas* (New York: Free Press, 1965); Bruce Robbins, ed., *Intellectuals: Aesthetics, Politics, Academics* (Minneapolis: University of Minnesota Press, 1990), esp. Stanley Aronowitz, "On Intellectuals," 3–56; and Russell Jacoby, *The Last Intellectuals: American Culture in the Age of Academe* (New York: Basic Books, 1987).

21. See Fraser and Freeman, *Audacious Democracy*, 4.

22. George Ross and I formed a working group in 1989 at Harvard's Center for European Studies to encourage comparative work on this question. For our formulation of the problem, see George Ross and Robert Fishman, "Changing Relationships between Labor and Intellectuals," *European Studies Newsletter* (Council for European Studies) (September/October 1989): 1–5. See also the excellent senior honors thesis of Harvard Social Studies student Paolo Di Rosa, working under my direction in 1986. Di Rosa's work is discussed in the next chapter.

23. This is not the place to discuss the Spanish Civil War and the extraordinary importance it took on for Hemingway, Orwell, and countless numbers of their contemporaries throughout the West.

24. On the democratic transitions and breakdowns, see nn. 2 and 3. On nondemocratic regimes, see Juan Linz, "Totalitarian and Authoritarian Regimes," in *Handbook of Political Science*, vol. 3: *Macropolitical Theory*, ed. Fred Greenstein and Nelson Polsby (Reading, Mass.: Addison-Wesley, 1975). For essays inspired by Linz's approach to comparative social science as well as previously unpublished essays by Linz himself, see the four-volume festschrift H. E. Chehabi, Richard Gunther, Scott

Mainwaring, and Alfred Stepan, eds., *Politics, Society, and Democracy* (Boulder, Colo.: Westview Press, 1993, 1995, 1998, 1999).

25. See Richard Gunther, "Spain: The Very Model of the Modern Elite Settlement," in *Elites and Democratic Consolidation in Latin America and Southern Europe*, ed. John Higley and Richard Gunther, 38–80 (Cambridge: Cambridge University Press, 1992). Doug McAdam, Sidney Tarrow, and Charles Tilly, *Dynamics of Contention* (Cambridge: Cambridge University Press, 2001).

26. On the Spanish model of regime transition and its contrast with other southern European cases, see Robert M. Fishman, "Rethinking State and Regime: Southern Europe's Transition to Democracy," *World Politics* 42, 3 (April 1990): 422–40. The contribution of pressure from below to this transition is a theme taken up by myself and others.

27. Much research clearly establishes the consistently high legitimacy of democracy in post-Franco Spain. For a comparative analysis, see José María Maravall, "Democracies and Democrats," in Maravall, *Regimes, Politics and Markets: Democratization and Economic Change in Southern Europe and Eastern Europe* (Oxford: Oxford University Press, 1997), 200–244; also, Leonardo Morlino and José Ramón Montero, "Legitimacy and Democracy in Southern Europe," in *The Politics of Democratic Consolidation: Southern Europe in Comparative Perspective*, ed. Richard Gunther, P. Nikiforos Diamandouros, and Hans-Jürgen Puhle, 231–60 (Baltimore: Johns Hopkins University Press, 1995); and the important contribution of Juan Linz and his collaborators at DATA, SA, Linz et al. *Informe sociológico sobre el cambio político en España 1975–1981 (Informe FOESSA)* (Madrid: Euramérica, 1981).

28. Víctor Pérez Díaz, *The Return of Civil Society: The Emergence of Democratic Spain* (Cambridge: Harvard University Press, 1993), 8, 43.

29. Peter McDonough, Samuel Barnes, and Antonio López Pina, *The Cultural Dynamics of Democratization in Spain* (Ithaca: Cornell University Press, 1998), 162.

30. See Susan M. Alberts, Jesús de Miguel, and Grover C. Jones III, "The Spanish Rompecabezas: Social Identity and Political Disaffection in Contemporary Spain," paper presented at the conference "From Isolation to Europe: Spain and Portugal in the European Union after Fifteen Years," Minda de Gunzburg Center for European Studies, Harvard University, November 2001.

31. Mariano Torcal, "Political Disaffection in New Democracies," paper presented at the seminar "Political Disaffection and Political Culture in European Democracies," Santiago de Compostela, Spain, October 19–21, 2000, 35.

32. It is worth noting that the most exceptional year in Spain's last two decades of labor conflict, 1988, with its highly successful nationwide general strike, lies outside the period I examine in table 1.1.

33. For work that emphasizes the social democratic, and thus left-oriented, components of PSOE policies, see the important works by Carles Boix, *Political Parties, Growth, and Equality: Conservative and Social Democratic Economic Strategies in the World Economy* (Cambridge: Cambridge University Press, 1998); Maravall, *Regimes, Politics, and Markets*; and Luiz Carlos Bresser Pereira, José María Maravall, and Adam Przeworski, *Economic Reforms in New Democracies: A Social-Democratic Approach* (Cambridge: Cambridge University Press, 1993).

For work that highlights disjunctions between the policies of PSOE Prime Minister Felipe González and traditional social democratic or socialist agendas, see the very useful discussion by Sebastian Royo, *From Social Democracy to Neoliberalism: The Consequences of Party Hegemony in Spain, 1982–1996* (New York: St. Martin's Press, 2000), as well as the important contribution of Sofía Pérez, *Banking on Priv-*

ilege: The Politics of Spanish Financial Reform (Ithaca: Cornell University Press, 1997).

For work that portrays the policies of the González era as more favorable toward business, see Donald Share, *Dilemmas of Social Democracy: The Spanish Socialist Workers Party in the 1980s* (New York: Greenwood, 1989).

34. Interview with CCOO leader, Puertollano, June 24, 1994.

35. For a conceptual argument developing this point, see Robert Fishman and Carol Mershon, "Workplace Leaders and Labour Organisation: Limits on the Mobilisation and Representation of Workers," *International Contributions to Labour Studies* 3 (1993): 67–90. See also chapter 2 in Fishman, *Working-Class Organization and the Return to Democracy in Spain.*

36. This observation is fundamentally different from the Olsonian free-rider formulation, which can encourage an overly simplistic view of collective action problems that fails to take note of the specific role of local leaders.

37. Of course, many intellectuals espouse religious faith as an integral part of their worldview. Furthermore, members of the clergy on occasion come to assume the role of "intellectual" for the larger society. I specify the secular component of intellectuals' socially recognized position to differentiate them from the clergy, who also occupy a position as recognized interpreters of reality, although in the case of the clergy it is a specific religious institution or community that affords them that status. Intellectuals may be religious or nonreligious in their worldview (and in the subcultural focus of their work), but their status as intellectuals in contemporary societies writ large is rooted in the secular world.

38. The multiple national and regional identities of Spaniards, and the complex attitudes, institutions, and policies reflecting this reality, represent an enormously important dimension of the country's post-Franco political experience. On this theme, see Linz and Stepan, *Problems of Democratic Transition and Consolidation,* 98–115. On the contrasts between Basque and Catalan nationalism, see Juan Diez Medrano, *Divided Nations: Class, Politics, and Nationalism in the Basque Country and Catalonia* (Ithaca: Cornell University Press, 1995).

39. This is the argument of Dietrich Rueschemeyer, Evelyne Huber Stephens, and John Stephens, *Capitalist Development and Democracy* (Chicago: University of Chicago Press, 1992). Most political sociologists would place somewhat less emphasis on the contribution of the working class to the emergence and consolidation of modern democratic regimes, but recent research continues to add to our knowledge on this question. On the contribution of labor to democratic transitions, see Ruth Berins Collier, *Paths toward Democracy: The Working Class and Elites in Western Europe and South America* (Cambridge: Cambridge University Press, 1999); and Samuel Valenzuela, "Labor Movements in Transitions to Democracy," *Comparative Politics* (July 1989): 445–73.

40. For an early sociological critique of such relatively loose understandings of the term, see Gary Alan Fine and Sherryl Kleinman, "Rethinking Subculture: An Interactionist Analysis," *American Journal of Sociology* 85 (July 1979): 1–20. See also Gary Alan Fine, "Small Groups and Culture Creation: The Idioculture of Little League Baseball Teams," *American Sociological Review* 44 (October 1979): 733–45.

41. See Wendy Griswold, *Cultures and Societies in a Changing World* (Thousand Oaks, Calif.: Pine Forge Press, 1994), 57.

42. See Lyn Spillman, *Nation and Commemoration: Creating National Identities in the United States and Australia* (Cambridge: Cambridge University Press, 1997), 6. Spillman's full formulation adds that cultures are "symbolic repertoires."

43. See Fine and Kleinman, "Rethinking Subculture."

44. These local leaders who belonged to a political party in one subculture and a union placed within the other subculture can be seen as the exception to the rule that political life typically clustered in one or the other of these two working-class traditions, both of them much transformed in the twentieth century.

Chapter 2. Exploring Social Ties

1. I use the terms *bond, tie, connection,* and *contact* interchangeably for stylistic relief. In a more monographic treatment of social connections themselves, a greater reliance on terminological distinctions would surely prove useful. For an interesting recent discussion of such terminological and conceptual issues, see David S. Hachen, *Sociology in Action* (Thousand Oaks, Calif.: Pine Forge Press, 2001), 12–31.

2. For excellent works offering a broad treatment of the methodological and conceptual issues posed by network analysis, see Alain Degenne and Michel Forse, *Introducing Social Networks,* trans. Arthur Borges (London: Sage, 1999), a volume that was first published, in 1994, in French; and Stanley Wasserman and Katherine Faust, *Social Network Analysis: Methods and Applications* (Cambridge: Cambridge University Press, 1994).

3. See James S. Coleman, *Foundations of Social Theory* (Cambridge: Harvard University Press, 1990), 300–321; Pierre Bourdieu, "The Forms of Capital," in *Handbook of Theory and Research for the Sociology of Education,* ed. John Richardson (Westport, Conn.: Greenwood Press, 1985).

4. These may be what network analysts call multiplex ties, that is, ties with multiple *contents;* alternatively, they may be ties with multiple *intellectuals.* However, from the standpoint of the sheer "volume" or content of interactions, in both cases the multiple-tie respondents maintain greater contact with intellectuals than do the single-tie respondents.

5. Among those respondents who clearly specified particular intellectuals with whom they maintained contact were leaders in the Nalón valley, Alcoi, and the Baix Llobregat, local contexts I discuss extensively in the next chapter.

6. For a useful introduction to this history in English, see Stanley Payne, *The Spanish Revolution* (New York: W. W. Norton, 1970).

7. For the most recent research on repression in the aftermath of the war as well as in its midst, see Santos Julia, Julián Casanova, Josep Maria Solé i Sabate, Joan Villarroya, and Francisco Moreno, *Victimas de la Guerra Civil* (Madrid: Temas de Hoy, 1999); and Julián Casanova, Francisco Espinosa, Conxita Mir, and Francisco Moreno Gómez, *Morir, matar, sobrevivir: La violencia en la dictadura de Franco* (Barcelona: Crítica, 2002).

8. I analyze this experience in Robert M. Fishman, *Working-Class Organization and the Return to Democracy in Spain* (Ithaca: Cornell University Press, 1990), chap. 4.

9. An important analysis of the anti-Franco opposition, which includes a highly useful discussion of the socialist opponents of the regime, is José Maravall, *Dictatorship and Political Dissent: Workers and Students in Franco Spain* (London: Tavistock, 1978). We will return to the theme of the socialist opposition in chapters 5 and 6.

10. Given the absence of any meaningful pattern of difference by subculture in this case, I have not reported the data in fig. 2.1 by that variable.

11. See Paolo Di Rosa, "The Disenchantment of Spanish Intellectuals: Reflections on the Relations between Intellectuals and Workers in Contemporary Spain," Social Studies honors thesis, Harvard College, November 1986.

12. Ibid., 74.

13. Interview with Alberto Rubio, CCOO Nalón valley headquarters, La Felguera de Langreo, July 1, 1994.

14. Di Rosa, "Disenchantment of Spanish Intellectuals," 89.

15. Ibid., 75.

16. Di Rosa, "Disenchantment of Spanish Intellectuals," provides an excellent and empirically grounded analysis of this process.

17. Ibid., 77, 109.

18. Interview with PCE local leaders, Mieres, April 25, 1994.

19. Interview with IU leaders, La Felguera de Langreo, July 4, 1994.

20. Interview with IU leader, Elda, May 24, 1994.

21. Interview with Severino Arias, Gijón, July 5, 1994.

22. See Di Rosa, "Disenchantment of Spanish Intellectuals," 105.

23. In some cases, ties may be the by-product of crossing paths in personal biographies rather than the result of the actors' specific interest, whether instrumental or intrinsic in nature, in building worker–intellectual connections.

24. For the sake of economy and clarity in presentation, I have omitted from fig. 2.8 the distinction of leaders with no ties, simple ties, or multiple ties. I report here the one contrast, by social ties of importance, for the analysis.

25. Interviews with Cesc Castellana, Sant Just de Llobregat, May 4–5, 1994.

Chapter 3. Social Ties and Discursive Horizons

1. Margaret Weir, "Urban Poverty and Defensive Localism," *Dissent* (summer 1994): 337–42.

2. Readers will be interested to note that only two of five surveyed local leaders in Linares maintained ties to intellectuals. The effort of Linares's workers and residents to save all existing jobs at the Santana Motor factory was extensively covered in Spain's national press. For a small sample of the immense list of newspaper articles on the conflict, see *El País*, February 20, 1994, 1, 50; March 5, 1994, 43; March 19, 1994, 21; April 17, 1994, 54; April 30, 1994, 43; and *El Mundo*, April 30, 1994, 73; May 8, 1994, 10.

3. On Langreo, see the work of geography professor and former mayor Aladino Fernández García, *Langreo: Industria, población, y desarrollo urbano* (Oviedo: Universidad de Oviedo, 1980).

4. See the thoughtful discussion on this point in Gary Marks, *Unions in Politics* (Princeton: Princeton University Press, 1989), 155–94.

5. Because the question under discussion was open-ended, the responses reported reflect the *relative* likelihood that leaders falling into different categories will engage in a given type of debate but not the *absolute* prevalence of each type of debate that is mentioned; in open-ended questions such as this one, the reported level of a phenomenon is lower than it would be in a closed-ended item. Without the prompt-

ing of a closed-ended question, many valid potential responses may never be articulated.

6. See the citations to these authors in chapter 1.

7. The twentieth-century history of Spain's labor movement includes two significant revolutionary episodes and several minor ones. The unsuccessful revolution of October 1934—during a period of conservative ascendancy in the context of the short-lived Second Republic—included the seizure of power by worker militants in Asturias for a period of several weeks. Two years later, in the midst of the broader Civil War, anarcho-syndicalist militants collectivized factories and other firms in Catalonia along with much agricultural land in Aragon. Although both episodes were defeated, they have remained present in the collective memory of labor activists.

8. I focus on the comparison between the two Asturian mining valleys that are near polar opposites in their linkage to—or isolation from—intellectuals. Langreo and San Martín, the two municipalities of the Nalón valley, report strong linkages to intellectuals. Seven of eight respondents in Langreo and six of seven respondents in San Martín reported ties to intellectuals. In Mieres, the largest municipality of the neighboring Caudal valley, only two of eight respondents reported ties to intellectuals. The contrast between two Valencian-region textile towns I examine is somewhat less stark. In Alcoi, seven of eight respondents report ties to intellectuals, and in neighboring Ontinyent four of seven respondents report ties. My focus in the Barcelona metropolitan area lies on a group sharing a common political origin rather than on a paired comparison of municipalities.

9. Much good work has been done on the history of the Asturian labor movement and on the challenges currently faced by Asturian society in the context of industrial decline and high unemployment. I have benefited especially from the work and insights of the historian Ruben Vega García. Among his writings, see *Crisis industrial y conflicto social: Gijón, 1975–1995* (Gijón: Ediciones Trea, 1998); and *La corriente sindical de izquierdas: Un sindicalismo de movilización* (Gijón: Ediciones de la Torre, 1991).

10. Among those who related this story were the Nalón valley leaders of the UGT, interview in Sama de Langreo, July 5, 1994, and of CCOO, interview in La Felguera de Langreo, July 1, 1994.

11. See "Jornadas sobre minería y su entorno," *El Entrego*, February 9, 10, 1990, mimeo, IU branch of San Martín del Rey Aurelio.

12. For the contribution of this historian on miners during the Franco period, see Ramón García Piñeiro, *Los mineros asturianos bajo el Franquismo* (Madrid: Fundación Primero de Mayo, 1990).

13. "Comunicado al pueblo de San Martín," mimeo, IU branch of San Martín del Rey Aurelio, 2.

14. See "Posibles caminos por un futuro esperanzador: Mesa redonda," November 7, 1990, mimeo, La Mesa de San Martín del Rey Aurelio. See p. 2 for the rhetorical question posed by Angel Manuel Arias.

15. "Concejo, informativo de I.U. de San Martín del Rey Aurelio," *Concejo*, 1993, mimeo, San Martín branch of IU, 2.

16. Interview with Alberto Rubio, Nalón valley headquarters of CCOO, La Felguera de Langreo, July 1, 1994.

17. Ibid., August 4, 1994.

18. *La Nueva España*, March 18, 1993, 16.

19. Interview with local CCOO leader, Mieres, July 3, 1994. I have renamed the leader Javier.

20. See the newspaper coverage in *La Nueva España*, July 1, 1994, 14.
21. Ibid., April 27, 1994, 21.
22. Ibid., April 25, 1994, 16.
23. Ibid., August 2, 1994, 14.
24. Ibid., August 4, 1994, 14.
25. Ibid., July 5, 1994, 17.
26. Ibid., July 4, 1994, 14 (emphasis added).
27. See, e.g., the efforts of retired socialist miner Severino Arias as he reported them to me during interviews in Gijón, July 4 and 5, 1994. Arias particularly lamented his inability to reorient the efforts of Turón activists in a more global direction.
28. The pragmatic and politically moderate profile of the Valencian region, which stands in stark contrast to the Asturian case, is manifested in many ways: lower levels of industrial conflict, more conservative voting patterns, lower union membership, and—in many local settings—cross-class understandings helping to support the region's large "underground" economy.
29. Interview with the secretary of the Ontinyent branch of EU (IU), July 11, 1995.
30. Interview with EU (IU) municipal representatives, July 10, 1995.
31. Ibid.
32. See "Document d'Esquerra Unida per al debat de l'estat de la ciutat: Un compromis amb el nostre poble," mimeo, Alcoi branch IU, December 1993, 23, 26.
33. The first two motions were presented on March 28, 1994; the third motion was presented on May 21, 1992.
34. Interview with the secretary general of CCOO in Alcoi, July 10, 1995.
35. Interview with Alcoi secretary general of CCOO, July 13, 1994.
36. Interview with Ontinyent secretary general of CCOO, July 13, 1994.
37. Interview with Ontinyent leader of IU, July 15, 1994.
38. Interview with Elda leader of IU, May 24, 1994.
39. On the opposition movement in the Baix Llobregat, see Ignasi Riera and José Botella, *El Baix Llobregat: 15 años de luchas obreras* (Barcelona: Blume, 1976). Also see Robert M. Fishman, *Working-Class Organization and the Return to Democracy in Spain* (Ithaca: Cornell University Press, 1990), chap. 4.
40. See Manuel Campo Vidal, "El Baix Llobregat: Una visio de Manuel Campo Vidal; Conferencia amb motiu de l'homenatge a Jaume Codina Vila al Centre de Promocio Economica del Prat, 22 de novembre de 1966," in *Materials del Baix Llobregat*, no. 3, pp. 105–9 (Sant Feliu de Llobregat: Centre d'Estudis Comarcals del Baix Llobregat, 1997), 106.
41. Dissertation research on this theme has been carried out by Lydia Fraile, Department of Political Science, Massachusetts Institute of Technology.
42. With the collapse of the Soviet Union and the eclipse of most West European communist parties in the late twentieth century, the democratic critique of Stalinism represented by Eurocommunism appears to have become a topic of largely historic interest, despite the strong passions elicited by this movement in the 1970s and thereafter. This is not the place to cite the large scholarly literature on Eurocommunism.
43. I witnessed this address by Emilio García in the closing stages of my research for *Working-Class Organization and the Return to Democracy in Spain*.
44. On the radicalism of the Barcelona labor movement in the early years of Spain's post-Franco democracy, and the contrast between that radicalism and the greater moderation of labor in Madrid, see Robert M. Fishman, "Divergent Paths:

Labor Politics in Barcelona and Madrid," in *Politics, Society, and Democracy: The Case of Spain*, ed. Richard Gunther (Boulder, Colo.: Westview Press, 1993).

45. On districtwide concertation in the Baix, see Kenneth A. Dubin, "La reconquesta comarcal: La política económica del Baix Llobregat en els anys democratics," 15–24, in *Materials del Baix Llobregat*, no. 3.

46. "Informe de la Comisión Ejecutiva a la Conferencia Comarcal," Cornellà de Llobregat, November 24, 1989, mimeo, 6, 7, 10.

47. This leaflet is available in the archives of the Fundació Utopía, Cornellà de Llobregat.

Chapter 4. Social Capital or Social Ties?

1. I presented the first version of this chapter in May 2000 at the departmental forum of the Department of Political and Social Sciences, Universitat Pompeu Fabra. A slightly revised version was given in October 2000 at the departmental colloquium of the Department of Sociology, University of Notre Dame. My thanks to Gosta Esping-Andersen, who served as discussant at the Pompeu Fabra forum; to Daniel Myers, who organized the Notre Dame colloquium; and to all those who offered comments in both settings.

2. In graduate courses at Yale in the later 1970s, Samuel Valenzuela offered this admonition, which he attributed to the distinguished Columbia sociologist Robert Merton.

3. See James Coleman, *Foundations of Social Theory* (Cambridge: Harvard University Press, 1990), 305. See also Alejandro Portes, "The Two Meanings of Social Capital," *Sociological Forum* 15, 1 (2000): 1–12; Alejandro Portes, "Social Capital: Its Origins and Applications in Modern Sociology," *Annual Review of Sociology* 24 (1998): 1–24; Michael Woolcock, "Social Capital and Economic Development: Toward a Theoretical Synthesis and Policy Framework," *Theory and Society* 27, 2 (1998): 151–208; Arnaldo Bagnasco, "Teoria del capitale sociale e political economy comparata," *Stato e Mercato*, no. 57 (December 1999): 351–72. See also the more recent critique by Stephen Samuel Smith and Jessica Kulynych, "It May Be Social, but Why Is It Capital? The Social Construction of Social Capital and the Politics of Language," *Politics and Society* 30, 1 (March 2002): 149–86.

4. See those cited in n. 3. Also see Robert Putnam, *Bowling Alone* (New York: Touchstone Books, 2001), in which Putnam reviews the surprisingly long history of usage of this term.

5. See Smith and Kulynych, "It May Be Social, but Why Is It Capital?"; and Vicente Navarro, "A Critique of Social Capital," paper delivered at the Annual Congress of Eastern Association of Social Sciences, Washington, D.C., February 22, 2002.

6. See Robert Putnam, with Robert Leonardi and Raffaella Nanetti, *Making Democracy Work: Civic Traditions in Modern Italy* (Princeton: Princeton University Press, 1993), chap. 6, appendix F, and 148–50; see also Putnam, *Bowling Alone*.

7. As serious quantitative methodologists will insist, nonsummed summary measures are available, but I argue that even such measures are not desirable in this case.

8. For a stimulating argument that money itself is not fully fungible as the result of culturally based social distinctions between different "monies," see Viviana Zelizer, *The Social Meaning of Money* (New York: Basic Books, 1994).

9. Smith and Kulynych, "It May Be Social, but Why Is It Capital?" 173.

10. See Barry Wellman, "Which Types of Ties and Networks Give What Kinds of Social Support?" in *Advances in Group Processes*, ed. Edward Lawler, Barry Markovsky, and Cecilia Ridgeway (Greenwich, Conn.: JAI Press, 1992), 9:207–35.

11. Mark Granovetter, *Getting a Job* (Cambridge: Harvard University Press, 1974). Also see Portes, "Social Capital."

12. See Bernice A. Pescosolido and Sharon Georgianna, "Durkheim, Suicide, and Religion: Toward a Network Theory of Suicide," *American Sociological Review* 54, 1 (February 1989): 33–48.

13. Theda Skocpol and Morris P. Fiorina, eds., *Civic Engagement in American Democracy* (Washington, D.C.: Brookings Institution Press; New York: Russell Sage Foundation, 1999); Robert Wuthnow, *Loose Connections: Joining Together in America's Fragmented Communities* (Cambridge: Harvard University Press, 1998).

14. See Peter A. Hall, "Social Capital in Britain," *British Journal of Political Science* 29 (1999): 417–61.

15. See Pamela Paxton, "Is Social Capital Declining in the United States? A Multiple Indicator Assessment," *American Journal of Sociology* 105, 1 (July 1999): 88–127.

16. See Mariano Torcal and José Ramón Montero, "La formación y consecuencias del capital social en España," *Revista Espanola de Ciencia Politica* 1, 2 (April 2000): 79–121. See also Torcal and Montero, "Facets of Social Capital in New Democracies: The Formation and Consequences of Social Capital in Spain," in *Social Capital and European Democracy*, ed. Jan W. van Deth, Marco Maraffi, Kenneth Newton, and Paul F. Whiteley, 167–91 (London: Routledge, 1999).

17. For a stimulating discussion on the fit between theories of collective action and the conceptualization of "social capital," see Jacint Jordana, "Collective Action Theory and the Analysis of Social Capital," in van Deth et al., *Social Capital and European Democracy*, 45–71.

18. James Baron and Michael Hannan, "The Impact of Economics on Contemporary Sociology," *Journal of Economic Literature* 32, 3 (September 1994): 1124.

19. On presidentialism versus parliamentarism, see Juan Linz and Arturo Valenzuela, eds., *The Failure of Presidential Democracy: Comparative Perspectives* (Baltimore: Johns Hopkins University Press, 1994); and Scott Mainwaring and Matthew Soberg Shugart, eds., *Presidentialism and Democracy in Latin America* (Cambridge: Cambridge University Press, 1997). On regime actors versus state actors, see Robert M. Fishman, "Rethinking State and Regime: Southern Europe's Transition to Democracy," *World Politics* 42, 3 (April 1990): 422–40; and Thomas Ertman, *Birth of the Leviathan: Building States and Regimes in Medieval and Early Modern Europe* (Cambridge: Cambridge University Press, 1997).

20. Samuel Huntington, *Political Order in Changing Societies* (New Haven: Yale University Press, 1969). Huntington argued that both the United States and the Soviet Union were fundamentally stable political systems characterized by strong institutions.

Chapter 5. Pursuing Alternative Explanations

1. A central assumption of the Weberian methodology for the social sciences— which I accept fully—is that explanations are in principle infinite in number, given the complex interconnections among processes and actors in the empirical world.

See Max Weber, "'Objectivity' in Social Science and Social Policy," in *The Methodology of the Social Sciences* (Chicago: Free Press, 1949), 49–112.

2. The difference is quite small and lacking in statistical significance at conventional levels.

3. This finding parallels the arguments of Kent Redding on the political import of social connections built through or outside institutions. See Kent Redding, *Making Race, Making Power: North Carolina's Road to Disenfranchisement* (Urbana: University of Illinois Press, 2003).

4. Much has been written on repression and opposition during the long decades of authoritarian rule. See Robert M. Fishman, *Working-Class Organization and the Return to Democracy in Spain* (Ithaca: Cornell University Press, 1990), chap. 4, esp. nn. 1 and 3. See also José María Maravall, *Dictatorship and Political Dissent: Workers and Students in Franco's Spain* (London: Tavistock, 1978); and Sebastian Balfour, *Dictatorship, Workers, and the City* (Oxford: Clarendon Press, 1989).

5. On the likelihood that participation in the opposition movement would lead to arrest, see the data in Fishman, *Working-Class Organization and the Return to Democracy in Spain*.

6. See Robert Putnam, *Bowling Alone* (New York: Touchstone Books, 2001).

7. Among the respondents who conveyed this sense were Francesc Castellana, Esplugues de Llobregat, May 4, 1994; and the interviewed IU leader in Elda, May 24, 1994.

8. IU interview in Alcoi, July 10, 1995.

9. Interviews with CCOO leader in Puertollano, June 24, 1994; and with IU leader in the same town also on June 24, 1994.

10. Mark Granovetter, *Getting a Job* (Cambridge: Harvard University Press, 1974), 35, 52.

11. An alternative methodological approach would be to use a series of interaction terms, instead of separate models by subculture, to test for differences in the causal dynamics at work in the two subcultures. I explored this possibility but ultimately rejected it (after running several such models and consulting with a number of methodologists) because the strategy I have used, with its reliance on separate models for the two subcultures, is substantively equivalent to the use of interaction terms but far easier to interpret if only because the use of interaction terms would have required a much longer list of independent variables in each model.

12. The odds ratio for this independent variable is 9.53 (significant at the .05 level) in socialist subculture model 2, in table 5.4. The tables presenting the logistic regression models do not list the odds ratios because they can be calculated from the reported coefficients.

13. Membership in a splinter group of the Socialist Party was also considered sufficient to be classified in the socialist subculture.

14. The odds ratio for this independent variable is 2.12 (significant at the .01 level) in postcommunist subculture model 1 and 2.07 (significant at the .01 level) in model 2 for the same subculture.

Chapter 6. The Specific and the General for the Social Scientist

1. As should be obvious, my measure of party membership includes all party members, both those sampled because of their institutional position as local party

leaders and other members sampled on the basis of their union leadership or their reputational leadership as reflected in the "snowball" stage of the sampling.

2. Interview with the mayor of Villena, May 24, 1994.

3. Interview with UGT leader in Sama de Langreo, July 5, 1994.

4. Those two academics must remain anonymous.

5. See Carles Boix, *Political Parties, Growth, and Equality: Conservative and Social Democratic Economic Strategies in the World Economy* (Cambridge: Cambridge University Press, 1998); José María Maravall, *Regimes, Politics, and Markets: Democratization and Economic Change in Southern and Eastern Europe* (Oxford: Oxford University Press, 1997); and Luiz Carlos Bresser Pereira, José María Maravall, and Adam Przeworski, *Economic Reforms in New Democracies: A Social Democratic Approach* (Cambridge: Cambridge University Press, 1993).

6. See the discussions in the already cited works by Donald Share, *Dilemmas of Social Democracy: The Spanish Socialist Workers Party in the 1980s* (New York: Greenwood Press, 1989); Sofía Pérez, *Banking on Privilege: The Politics of Spanish Financial Reform* (Ithaca: Cornell University Press, 1997); Sebastián Royo, *From Social Democracy to Neoliberalism: The Consequences of Party Hegemony in Spain, 1982—1996* (New York: St. Martin's Press, 2000); as well as the nuanced view of Paul Heywood, *The Government and Politics of Spain* (New York: St. Martin's Press, 1995).

7. Rafael Ribó made this argument when I interviewed him in Barcelona, July 25, 1994.

8. Interview with Severino Arias, Gijón, July 4, 1994.

9. Interview with UGT leader, Sama de Langreo, July 5, 1994.

10. Interview in Oviedo, July 6, 1994.

11. Paolo Di Rosa, "The Disenchantment of Spanish Intellectuals: Reflections on the Relations between Intellectuals and Workers in Contemporary Spain," Social Studies honors thesis, Harvard College, November 1986, 115.

12. Leonardo Morlino, *Democracy between Consolidation and Crisis* (Oxford: Oxford University Press, 1998), 175, 177.

13. For an important work on the anti-Franco opposition and the socialist role within it, see José Maravall, *Dictatorship and Political Dissent: Workers and Students in Franco Spain* (London: Tavistock, 1978).

14. See Robert M. Fishman, *Working-Class Organization and the Return to Democracy in Spain* (Ithaca: Cornell University Press, 1990).

15. For an analysis of the impact of the Catalan context itself on the opinions of labor activists, see Robert M. Fishman, "Divergent Paths: Labor Politics in Barcelona and Madrid," in *Politics, Society, and Democracy: The Case of Spain*, ed. Richard Gunther (Boulder, Colo.: Westview Press, 1993).

16. On the conflict between the PSOE and the UGT, see Royo, *From Social Democracy to Neoliberalism*; Javier Astudillo, *Los recursos del socialismo: Las cambiantes relaciones entre el PSOE y la UGT (1982–1993)* (Madrid: Instituto Juan March, 1998); and Katryna Burgess, *Parties and Unions in the New Global Economy* (Pittsburgh: University of Pittsburgh Press, 2003).

17. See, most recently, Doug McAdam, Sidney Tarrow, and Charles Tilly, *Dynamics of Contention* (Cambridge: Cambridge University Press, 2001), on this issue.

18. I am indebted to Sidney Tarrow for suggesting this point.

Chapter 7. Beyond These Towns and Valleys

1. David Held, "The Transformation of Political Community: Rethinking Democracy in the Context of Globalization," in *Democracy's Edges*, ed. Ian Shapiro and Casiano Hacker-Cordon, 84–111 (Cambridge: Cambridge University Press, 1999), 106, 108.

2. See Jon Elster, ed., *Deliberative Democracy* (Cambridge: Cambridge University Press, 1998).

3. Mabel Berezin, "Politics and Culture: A Less Fissured Terrain," *Annual Review of Sociology* 23 (1997): 361–83.

4. Stephen Hart, *Cultural Dilemmas of Progressive Politics: Styles of Engagement among Grassroots Activists* (Chicago: University of Chicago Press, 2001).

5. See Sidney Tarrow, "Rooted Cosmopolitans: Transnational Activists in a World of States," paper presented at the Kellogg Institute, University of Notre Dame, March 2, 2003; and Sidney Tarrow and Doug McAdam, "Scale Shift in Transnational Contention," paper presented at the conference "Transnational Process and Social Movements," Bellagio, Italy, July 22–26, 2003.

6. I discuss important differences between Spain and Portugal along this dimension in Robert M. Fishman, "Rethinking Iberian Democracy Twenty-Five Years after the Transitions," paper presented at the Annual Meeting of the American Political Science Association, Boston, August 2002.

7. For a stimulating collection of essays on the political role of intellectuals, see Charles Lemert, ed., *Intellectuals and Politics: Social Theory in a Changing World* (Newbury Park, Calif.: Sage, 1991).

8. Dick Flacks, "Making History and Making Theory: Notes on How Intellectuals Seek Relevance," 3–18, in Lemert, *Intellectuals and Politics*, 16.

9. Christopher Lasch, *The Revolt of the Elites and the Betrayal of Democracy* (New York: Norton, 1995), 117.

10. Interview with CCOO leader, Ontinyent, July 13, 1994.

11. See the poem published in a public school newspaper, quoted as the epigraph to chapter 1 of this book.

Index

Page numbers followed by *f* or *t* refer to figures and tables respectively.